SACHEVERELL SITWELL
Photograph by Christopher Barker

AN INDIAN SUMMER

An Indian Summer

100 RECENT POEMS BY

Sacheverell Sitwell

MACMILLAN LONDON

ISBN boards 0 333 33474 4
ISBN paper 0 333 33475 2

First published 1982 by
MACMILLAN LONDON LIMITED
4 Little Essex Street London WC2R 3LF
and Basingstoke
Associated Companies in Auckland, Dallas, Delhi, Dublin,
Hong Kong, Johannesburg, Lagos, Manzini, Melbourne,Nairobi,
New York, Singapore, Tokyo, Washington and Zaria

Printed and bound in Great Britain
at The Pitman Press, Bath

Contents

Musicalia

Harlequinade

For a Floral Inebriation

Pomona

A Bestiary of Birds and Beasts

Preface

A little more than half a century ago, while I was still neglecting my education at Oxford, Sacheverell Sitwell's *Southern Baroque Art* first introduced me to his creative talents. On the fly-leaf of an orange-clad copy, which has followed me through the years from bookshelf to bookshelf, and, indeed, across the globe, I see that I have written, in a script I can hardly recognise today, 'Renishaw August 1925'. That summer, staying with the three young poets and their strange and memorable parents Sir George and Lady Ida Sitwell, I suppose I must have opened it. I was immediately dazzled; and the section I found most captivating was the chapter entitled 'The King and the Nightingale', the story of how the mad and melancholic Philip V of Spain, grandson of the 'Roi Soleil', was restored to real life by the exquisite skill of the great *castrato* singer Farinelli, who sang him the same four songs every night during the next two decades, thus presumably repeating them some three thousand six hundred times, to an audience that consisted of the King and Queen alone.

What delighted me even more than author's brilliant descriptions of Baroque art and architecture – I had been brought up in a household that preferred the Gothic mode – were his soaring poetic flights, his constant rush of ideas and his headlong flow of imagery, as when he evoked the choir of Spanish nightingales who populated the palace gardens and conspired to keep the unhappy King awake, or the cruel invasion of the Sun, who, further to trouble his mind, came leaping lion-like through his bedroom-window. True, there were learned passages, devoted to the general history of the period, that temporarily held up the narrative; but the tale of the curious relationship between the invalid French sovereign and the tall and solid Neapolitan eunuch triumphantly carried them along; and I soon became an ardent follower of my new friend's prose style, which, having begun to write a book myself, I did my best to imitate, with, alas, extremely poor results.

Southern Baroque Art appeared in 1924; and Sacheverell Sitwell, according to *Who's Who*, has since published almost seventy books on an extraordinary range of subjects – from his own travels, his favourite musicians and painters, and the flowers he loves, Austrian rococo monasteries and churches, Khmer temples, Japanese landscapes, gardens and shrines, and that mysterious phenomenon the British poltergeist, to the huge visionary surveys of past and present he once jokingly called his 'oratorios'. These are only a few of the topics he has chosen as a literary spring-board; but, whatever his point of departure may be, his detours *en route* are usually no less interesting than the conclusion that he reaches. They exhibit both a richly stocked mind and a highly developed sensibility. He bears not the slightest resemblance I can distinguish to any other modern writer.

Oddly enough, one of his literary ancestors is a famed Victorian prophet.

Though he considers Ruskin a 'thoroughly scatter-brained' sage, in some respects he has adopted Ruskin's method – that of imaginative association, which enables him to glide from theme to theme, and give a vivid autobiographical colouring to every new idea he introduces. But then, despite his achievements as a prose-writer, Sacheverell Sitwell is primarily a poet; and it is hard to understand why his volume of *Collected Poems*, published in 1936, should have had no successor till the present day. He ceased writing poetry for a decade, and it was only in 1972 that he started issuing a series of privately printed pamphlets, each containing a handful of works he thought particularly worth attention; and these pamphlets have provided most of the material that has been assembled here. The book's title, *An Indian Summer*, suggests its origin and contents. Many of these poems are retrospective; the poet looks back, recognises how much he has lost, yet discovers how little change his deepest interests and affections show, and how close the distant past still seems. Some especially moving poems are dedicated to his beloved sister Edith, who once read him verses in the low-ceilinged nursery at Renishaw and first encouraged him to write, and the guardian of whose memory he feels that he has now become. His brother Osbert also reappears, latterly a crippled and frustrated figure, as does the background of their youth, their old home, with its bluebell woods and faintly smoke-grimed statues and the industrial netherland of pit-heads and chimneys that has submerged the valley beneath Sir George's park.

Yet human experience, he reflects in 'An Old Snapshot' – a portrait of the octogenarian artist when he was still four or five years old – despite all its vicissitudes, endlessly repeats itself. We inhabit a circular universe:

> A round world,
> > or it comes round in a circle,
> As you can see it in the snapshot,
> As round as the 'round O' of the wooden playhouse,
> > and all of life played in it,
> Or foretold there.

Even as a child he was already fascinated by audible and visual beauty; and few writers, in a lifetime of listening and looking, have followed beauty with such devoted care. He believes, he tells us, that he now examined nearly all surviving works of art, heard most of the music and seen the majority of great pictures; and he might have added that, wherever he has visited a fresh landscape, he has paid affectionate attention to its native flowers and trees; and that flowers, English or foreign, wild or cultivated, are among his ruling passions.

The poems published in *An Indian Summer* may be divided roughly into three main groups – those which recall the past, his sister's memory and the life they used to share, and sound, now and then, an angry note; those which describe the passing of time and the sorrows of old age –

> I am as someone waiting outside a house to get in,
> Not wanting to go home, but it is late and pours with rain
> > and no one will open a window and throw down a key

– and, finally, the largest group, which celebrate the splendours of the natural world and the saving powers of Art.

In a short preface I cannot attempt to discuss either the poet's professional technique or the influence of other poets who may have helped perhaps to shape his work. It must be enough to say that, besides his sister Edith, Arthur Waley, an old and dear friend, brilliant translator of Chinese and Japanese texts, and a master of rhythmic free verse, may have provided an inspiriting example; and that some of his poems bear a certain resemblance to Waley's delightful renderings of the ninth-century Chinese poet Po Chü-I. One notices the same subtle, unforced music, the same engagingly colloquial touches, the same digressive pattern of ideas and feelings, in which the writer seems to be not only addressing the reader, but quietly talking to himself. *An Indian Summer* is an exceedingly personal record of Sacheverell Sitwell's long creative life – so personal that many references may escape the uninstructed critic. If he is sometimes obscure, his obscurity is not of the kind that had become fashionable since the days of T. S. Eliot and Ezra Pound; and, possibly for this reason Sitwell is nowadays a much neglected poet, seldom mentioned by contemporary reviewers. I hope that the publication of *An Indian Summer* will restore him to the place that he deserves.

Peter Quennell

Looking for the Gods of Light

On a reading of *Hamlet, Prince of Denmark*, Act 1, Scene 5

I find thee apt;
And duller should'st thou be than the fat weed
That rots itself in ease on Lethe's wharf,
Would'st thou not stir in this.

Of all ghostly converse
    this the most famous and most chilling,
In an actor's voice, remember!
    And I accept the challenge:—
For who is there who has not dreamt of the dead?
A young boy can dream of a dead animal,
    a puppy dog that died,
Now inhabitant of Sirius the dog-star,
    and yapping, yapping, yapping on that excoriated shore

But 'apt'? What for? Wherefore, and why?
    Above all, why is he choosing me?
Why has he picked on me?
Apt? In the dict: 'suitable, prompt, quick-witted',
    and again 'prompt',
'To suggest, help out an actor,
Or speaker by reading his next words,
    or suggesting words'
So we are back again on the stage or in the theatre
    with the ghost, no less, of Hamlet's brother

I had certainly that odd experience
    on the last night I will ever sleep in my childhood home,
And feeling and knowing this at the time:—
When the footsteps came up and down again
    in the inverse direction one would have imagined
Outside our door.
No. Not my brother who is dead,
    who must have set foot, even trodden may be the fat weed
On Lethe's wharf,

But his alter ego and intendant
    with all his faults and little else to boast of!
Why should he be coming up,
    then coming down again, instead of going upstairs to bed,
What for, and why?
    Having heard stories of just such footsteps ever since I was a child
Along that passage and passing that very door:—
It made our hearts stand still:—
While we waited, waited,
    wondering what would happen next!

Nothing: of course nothing,
    there was no more to come:—
And so indeed what was it all about?
We will not know, if ever
    till we come ourselves
With creaking of Charon's rowlocks,
    that rattle like chains or like handcuffs,
To 'the fat weed that rots itself in ease on Lethe's wharf'

An Old Snapshot

A little boy four or five years old,
    standing legs wide apart, walking-stick in left hand,
Handkerchief in coat pocket,
Keeping still for a moment in time
    that was marked on every clock and watch,
And then moved on.

Waiting to have his picture taken
    on the broad pavement of The Crescent
Which curves round behind him
    towards the house where he was born;
And looking at the world in front of him
    that comes round full circle,
Even in the snapshot,
And will come round behind him
    and reach to where he stands,
With the laburnum tree across the road behind the railings
    that he used to climb into,
But it is not likely to be there still after all these years.

A round world,
    or it comes round in a circle,
As you can see it in the snapshot,
As round as the 'round O' of the wooden playhouse,
    and all of life played in it,
Or foretold there.

My mother was young then,
    and I am wondering whether she ever had a camera,
It would be unlike her!
But the little boy stands outside a friend's house
    who probably took the photograph.

My uncle and aunt had a summer villa across The Crescent,
    while we lived at the time
In another house further down and out of sight,
Which we kept until I was so ill in the winter of 1919–1920
    and indeed thought myself that I was dying,
Having written half-a-dozen pages of my first prose book
    before I was taken ill.

We sold the house after I had recovered
    and I was never there again:—
But my imagination if ever I had one
    was born climbing on the rock-pools
And walking on those sands.

Ballad: 'The Hyacinth that was Dying'
(from an old slum song)

The little boy was crying
To his hyacinth that was dying
No other little boy along the long street
Has a hyacinth
Tears pour down
The little boy's cheeks like rain
Rain pours
Like tears down the windowpane
No other sight
No other sound in the world
But rain rain
Rain

On the canal
Where he fishes for minnows with a twisted pin
It rains and rains
Rain rain
On trolley-bus and ominous aeroplane

'And his mother tells him
His hyacinth will grow again'
No good no good
In the long hours of rain

Swan Walk, 1918

Across the road was the walled garden
    with the mulberry tree,
The dirty, foggy Thames ran along one side
    and the War was 'still on';
It was like that,
    and we knew all the painters and the poets

And now, still trying,
    for it is a lifetime ago,
Have I caught or let fall the Leonids?
There could be a little of the meteor dust upon my fingers,
    no more than that,
And it is all

'Oh! that love and time'

Oh! that love and time
Could be kept fast in a locket,
And to forget illness and infirmity
    and growing old,
And be rejoined with the things I loved
    that interest me:—
Where age is concerned

I am as someone waiting outside a house to get in,
Not wanting to go home, but it is late and pours with rain
    and no one will open a window and throw down the key.

So to work again to poems just begun
    and as ever interrupted,
Building a house for Pholus the Centaur
    for that was my fantasy of the moment,
And having trouble with it
    in designing a bed of straw for the Centaur
Half-man, half-horse to lie down in and sleep comfortably.

Remembering a story told by a friend,
    a young poet as it happened,
Impecunious as of tradition and travelling in Greece
    deep into Arcadia to visit the Temple of Bassae,
The work of Ictinos architect of the Parthenon;
    where in default of an inn of any sort
He had to spend the night in a shepherd's hut
    where they regaled him with stories of hauntings by the Centaurs,
Who were to be seen in the moonlight
Striking sparks with their hoofs in playfulness
    upon the temple steps.

Diverted thence to the Sharawaggi Kingdom
    of dragon finials and white orchid petals in the bee-black hair,
Which assayed,
    I return to an earlier predilection
For the chamber music, as though mullioned, wainscotted,
Of John Lyly's 'While Cupid and Campaspe played
    At cards for kisses',
Wondering if put to it how to complete the poem worthily:—
Having tried my hand at the minor, if not lesser keys,
    long, long ago
In the six poems for *Exalt the Eglantine,*
And in half a century the poems should not stale and wither:
    it is the hand that ages, not the ink upon the paper:—
And now,
    inconsequential as ever
I am of mind to go blackberrying.

Eclogue Obstiné

Not liking
    the athletes and the satyrs on Greek vases,
Nor over much their temples

Not caring
    for the youths who stood under the stone pines
With their trainers and admirers,
Their skins oiled and powdered with red or yellow,
    or other 'of the five kinds of recommended dust'

Preferring
    to tread on lambskins as soft as sleep
To a bed of fresh cut vine-strippings,
    and the nymph-guardian of the pool;
Oread from the gentian'd hills,
Dryad,
    or potamid of the pebbled riverbed;
What do I care!
While a horned face looks in through the window,
    and the pool of moonlight moves across the floor

Ballad: The Two Waltzes

Set the scene for a summer night in Paris
From every quarter of the town
Let there come laughter and clinking of wine-glasses
As when Métella sups with Baron Gondremarck
And the orchestra of the Café Riche
Plays back her waltz to her
Immortal moment
Music within music
Immortal moment that I have known too
But will not tell of it . . .
. . . That was in the time I was a poet
For when young I was to net the Leonids

But the world is not as I would have it be . . .
Now with hideous stereoscopic pictures in the doorway
That smile or rather leer as you look at them
Like an evil vision on a biscuit-tin
Among the sky-signs
And horrible high houses of Montmartre
All dead now. A dead city. A city of dead rats
It seems to me

. . . And I know the double image of Italy
In her beauty and her hopelessness
If I think of Italian airs Italian graces
It is to know her music
And how a flower of music
Forms in the air
     and falls to nothing . . .
The slums of Naples are built as though on purpose
Not to look out upon the Siren Bay
Their eyes are turned inward upon their own sores
Yet the ruin of Naples is her carnations and mandolines
And now the poison I warned against
Begins to take effect on me

There is poetry for the sake of poetry
And for no other reason.
Listen! listen! to how beautiful those songs can be . . .
Music which we love for the sake of music
. . . Last night was the episode of the flower-seller
Who came to our table with roses and Parma violets
. . . Buying violets
And burying our faces in them
And the violets had water on them
Tap water. But it had been shaken on them
By nymphs
     the scent of the dark violets
Was like the temples of a nymph and her wet forehead
The mauve violets as the scent of a nymph's cheekbones
When they climb out of the pool
And the white
     like nymphs too wet to hold . . .

'Tell me, Daphne'

Tell me,
    Daphne,
Daughter of the green river,
    turned into a laurel
(though I prefer an ilex tree),
Tell me,
    in which Elysium it is to be

Lovely changeling,
    only for a few moments
For no longer
    than the jet-plane passes overhead;
But it would be to live through all the centuries,
    then be for ever dead

Revenant

Why do you not come to me more often,
    white scent and loveliness of the white syringa,
As last night?
    It matters not how sad you make me

Coming in from the orchard where were the white lilacs;
    and there was rain on your cheeks,
And on the green cheeks of the apples,
    for you had been riding

Why is it less and less,
    as to one long left in prison,
And forgotten?

The ravishment of the white rose again,
    lying under me,
Who was all fire within her
    and into deeper sleep with no awakening

Nymph of the Bluebell Wood

There were collieries all round when I was a child
    and the molten tip put the night sky on fire,
For nymph or fauness by the light of that;
    and after,
Number the bluebells and soon tire

Woods that were one blue flame of love,
    as I have told,
But I was too young then,
    and now I am too old

'Listen, sweet hyacinth'

Listen,
    sweet hyacinth,
The flower and the scent,
Virgin and courtesan,
Maiden,
With no impediment

I would know the truth,
My hyacinth,
Matchless flower and
Hyacinth of my demi-youth,
Now I have passed the meridian
And move towards the shades

Fair flower,
That gives of herself,
I would know where you have been
So tell me, tell me!
That in the underworld
(All I can hope for)
I may be a shadow
Where you are seen

A Waist of Sandalwood

Shade
Pied yellow and white with broken petals
And now an unpillaged frangipani

Not the red sort
     nor that which lily-white
Seems stained with its own pollen

But the white and sacrosanct
Of flesh of a cracked claw
     consistence

Of crustacean flesh
     soft-shelled
From sweetwater pools of contentment

Where
     a waist of sandalwood
Splashed with her own shadow in the water coolness

The same
That wore the frangipani
In her bee-black hair

Silenus from a Silver Tetradrachm

Sicily
And slopes of Aetna
Before the cactus or the orange
But with the vine the pine
The olive and the oleander

Goat-ear
With shining scalp
Tidy hair fringe round the nape of the neck

You are half-drunk
I saw you under the black grapes
Later where blue morning-glory climbs
Upon the white cabin
Pretending to beg for water
But looking in through the square window

Goat-ear and tramp-philosopher
What am I to wish for you this fiery autumn?
That Dorcion comes past and shows her naked thigh
O sip of snow and sip of honey!
Or that you thrust into a heart of fire
And sleep upon a threshing-floor
Silenus
You are a danger to both sexes

Ballad: 'Sous un ciel chagrin'

(from a woodcut by Sharaku)

Thoughts are leaden
Leaden
As the lovers move past
And he leads her
Air is like lead
And dark like mica

Ah! what foreboding
In their every movement
The man's concern in her
His looking
Looking in her face
And leading her

Her sleepwalking
Or drifting movement
Drifting
Under a sky like lead
To bloodshed
And their double coffins

'The Turn of the World'

(an old folk phrase for the time between dark and dawn)

In the turn of the world,
In the hour between dark and dawn,
Of what am I thinking?
No longer young now,
And having looked and heard so much,
I wonder—
Does one not wonder?—
Where are we going?
There is nothing to be sure of,
That is certain.

There is only the beauty of the world,
Not yet blighted,
And which may turn to anything.
Ah! in this little hour
Let us walk in the dawn
And wet our dew strings,
A countryman's phrase
In shepherd's language;
If it is not the false dawn
And a white ash is falling.

Looking for the Gods of Light

1

Now the message is
    to enjoy ourselves,
And look for such there be,
    dead or alive, the Gods of Light:—
And riding this corpus of what is already written
    we 'take off' from the mother-body,
The 'boost' causing us to accelerate

But where to go in time?
And where in space?

Since it entails no more than sitting before a sheet of paper,
Why not to watch a pair of eagles,
        of 'bald-head' eagles;
They join feet high in air,
        and then fall together
Twisting over and over,
        'depth of dive perhaps a thousand feet',
Spiralling together with interlocked claws
        to their own pleasure,
But alarm and consternation of all other birds,
        and all just for a breath of air

2

But it would be unwise to expect too much.
        or indeed anything at all in human terms
Of the nuptial flight,
        or love-play of eagles in their chasm between the mountains:—
Just as, to descend to bathos,
        it was decidely a mercy to the human race
That l'Aiglon, son of Napoleon and King of Rome died young,
        before the wars started all over again because of him

So many wonderful beings or Gods of Light
        are born of insignificant parents;
There is at most sometimes a predisposition in the same direction
        towards what the son accomplishes:—
A humble watchmaker, shall we say,
        produces a Thomas Tompion of whom even in the name
We hear the chiming of his workshop full of clocks

Only last week
        a famous musician and conductor
Said he knew he would fall dead
        were he to meet Mozart face to face walking in the street,
Which is a measure of how we should revere the dead
        and wish to join ourselves with them
In the eternal darkness,
        which is at the same time all light
And no darkness,
        nothing but light
In our conscious thinking of them

13

The transfer of talent coming more often from adoption,
   meaning long training since childhood,
With if possible no other schooling,
   than from direct inheritance in blood;
As with the Italian *quattro* and *cinquecento*,
   to think only of their names,
Raffaello, Michelangelo, Leonardo,
   Palladio, son of Piero dalla Gondola, and so on,
Which inspire more than do the names of great soldiers or kings

But that was Italy of *la bella mano*,
   and the very softness of the Italian is its undoing,
For the rough guttural of the Hollander
   was no less prolific in its one generation,
While is it only fortuitous that no poet has had pupils?
   Though it is certainly true that one must learn to write poetry
      by teaching oneself,
And how different that must be from being apprenticed to a sculptor,
   a drudge in the icy studio of a second Nollekens,

One would want to write poems when young,
   and again when old,
Keeping perhaps the poetry to oneself
   as one's last relics,
Which I am trying to effect in my own person,
   having enjoyed notoriety while I was young,
And no longer needing or wanting criticism
   now that I am old.

No More

The Octogenarian

'The octogenarian'
    (come November!)
'Leaned from his window,
To the valerian
Growing below
Said, "My nightcap
Is only the gap
In the trembling thorn
Where the mild unicorn
With the little Infanta
Danced the lavolta
(Clapping hands: molto
Lent' eleganta)"'

While this other
Octogenarian
Who is your brother
None other
Sits here at his window
Where, if the rest of you would care to know,
He has been thinking and writing
Long before most of you were born

A quoi bon? Who cares?
Not I,
Who am here remembering,
While the days rush by
And the long night is looming

Thinking just now
What an exciting world it was
When the three of us were young together:—
Even in trouble for being young
    and having talent:—
Well! it is over and finished now,
    long ago,
And will never be again

So up to 'the fourth floor high in air'
Where you my sister lived for eighteen years,
Writing some of your best and most individual poems
In a vein of fantasy that never slackened
Or abated;
Written quickly,
Even effortlessly it seemed,
To have the music fitted to them

Let me hear the barrel-organ,
      that played on Saturday afternoons in Moscow Road,
It matters not how banal the tune:
Let it be 'When Irish eyes are smiling',
      and I am back with you
On a blazing June evening in 1921 or 1922.
There seemed to be a new poem of yours
      to read to us,
Almost every time we came to see you,
And climbed the four double-flights of stone stairs
      up to your flat:—
Poems in a vein of fantasy
      invented for yourself,
And all your own,
      like nothing else before or since

Excepting, I have often thought,
      a resemblance, even a kinship
To the *Balli di Sfessania* of Jacques Callot,
Who in the staid language of the dictionary of painters
      ran away from home at Nancy in Lorraine
And went to Rome,
'Some time between 1608–11*, aged fifteen or sixteen',
Having joined the Gypsies, or at least frequented
      fairgrounds and the encampments of nomad actors:—
Jacques Callot being a youth of the precocity
      and youthful genius
Of the child Rimbaud another native of Lorraine

Of which experiences
      expressed in fantasy
The *Balli di Sfessania* are the memory;
A frontispiece and twenty-three little woodcuts of dancing
      figures

* Within the lifetime of Shakespeare, as long ago as that.

no more than three or four inches high;
Giving the impression, I have tried to express it,
    as though he made the woodcuts using the point of his
  knife
Upon anything he could find,
    a wooden bench, the corner of a trestle-stage or
  kitchen table:—
And most improbably made the prints for them there and
  then,
    using what scraps of paper came to hand

Should one see all thirty-seven poems of *Façade*
    printed close together on a theatre or concert
  programme,
The images jump at the eye off the crowded page
    in a strength of originality only reminiscent
Of the little woodcuts of the *Balli di Sfessania*

How then my sister
    did you arrive at your extraordinary imagery,
Who had no visual sense, no visual curiosity?
Having only begun to write poems
    at twenty-six or seven years old,
And so in your early thirties by 1921 or 1922;
Writing your poems in bed in the early morning
    in your bedroom looking out at the back,
From which I even remember the dismal view?

'Under influence' certainly from music,
    of Debussy more particularly,
Though Mozart I remember always irritated you,
    you did not like to admit it for my sake
But thought him 'too Italianate';
And at that time in those years
    we all had the 'Russian' tunes of *Petrouchka* in our ears
I can hear them now
Intermingling with whiskey-smeared tears of Erin
    from the slow Irish slum-waltz down in the street
  below

Let us stay up here for a few more moments,
    before it is all pulled down
The chance may never come again!
The block of flats was demolished
    bulldozed long, long years ago

The best of your individual poems,
    Such as 'Long steel grass,'
Preluded by that magical fanfare
    the composer and I heard played on a trumpet
By an itinerant fortune-teller in the streets of Catania:—
The best of the individual poems,
    I reiterate,
Being more than a little of a mystery
    as to their source and origin:
'Cried the navy-blue ghost
Of Mr. Belaker
The allegro Negro cocktail-shaker'

    or

'In a room of the palace
Black Mrs. Behemoth
Gave way to wroth
And the wildest malice,'

    or

'Across the flat and the pastel snow
Two people go . . . "And do you remember
When last we wandered this shore?" . . . "Ah no!
For it is cold hearted December." '

The best of her poems,
    I repeat,
Remain more than a little of a mystery:—
Being no less mysteriously put to music
    in so inimitable a fashion
By a youth of genius not yet twenty years old:—
    No lover of poetry in particular,
But he worked instinctively I remember,
    as if blindfolded or even under a spell,
And as though led or guided:—
The poems themselves,
    that is the wonder of his partnership with my sister,
Being, as has been said, like nothing else before or since

I am remembering an afternoon
    like this one, or another one,
When she read us:
    'Daisy and Lily,

Lazy and silly,
Walk by the shore of the wan grassy sea, —'
And again:
'Lily O'Grady,
Silly and shady,
Longing to be
A lazy lady,
Walked by the cupolas, gables in the
Lake's Georgian stables',
Or, for an encore:
'Rose Castles
Those bustles
Beneath parasols seen!'

And I know it is incongruous,
    but in their femininity
They only match the masculine virility
    of the little woodcuts of the Rimbaud-youth,
Jacques Callot

But it 'sensibly darkens' a little
    and time to be going home to Carlyle Square,
Till we come back again in three or four days' time
    to hear more of the poems,
And how the music goes with them?

They make for themselves a little niche in time
    that I have tried to halt for a moment
On a hot June evening in Bayswater all those years ago,
So that you can hear her happy laughter in her poems,
    and see her as I have often written of her,
Long and thin and tall and aquiline,
    like no one we will ever see again:—
Before we throw down a coin
    from the window
And the barrel-organ moves on
    into receding time

While the octogenarian,
    myself,
Is still at my window
    thinking of her and hearing that haunting fanfare
Till no one remembers
    and soon it will be:—
'The man with the lanthorn

19

Peers high and low;
Not more
Than a snore
As he peers high and low'

No More

Why
    cannot I walk into the wood
We called the wilderness,
Beyond the statues of the warrior and the amazon?
Why
    cannot I walk into the wood
Through the wooden gate
    where I was often frightened as a child,
And look down to the lake between the trees?

It is true I never saw the bluebells
    till I had left school,
I was never there in May or June,
But,
    why can I not walk into the bluebell wood,
Be young again
    and come back into the house of tragic memories?

Come back
    and find her living
In her years of genius
    who is dead now,
Before the shadows lifted,
    and darker shadow fell!

Walk into the wood of bluebells
    that once
Were one blue flame of love:—
Sad thoughts,
    sad thoughts again,
I cannot tell

Schlaflos (Sleepless)

Tall spectre and shadow,
    too tired to talk,
Wheeled in
    with the huge rings on your transparent hands,
In the mid-dark of your long nights of weakness
You called out in your sleep for one who loves you,
    who is mine by love, not yours by blood;
And I know you go back to the night-light darkness
    in the low ceilinged nursery
Which you had not long left when I remember you,
In the North Bow Room looking out on dark old trees,
    up Mosborough Hill towards black Sheffield
And next door to it our day-nursery
With the wooden rocking-horse on the sloping cement floor outside,
    Where that other now an invalid,
Shared his red-currant ice with me on August evenings
Oh! how long ago!
And later when I was a little older
    it was the bedroom of my tutor Colonel Fantock
Ah! what can I say about it all!

My brother had his little room across the passage,
    and mine was the bedroom next to it now a china-cupboard,
Where I was so ill with appendicitis before going back to school;
I remember looking out with him over the garden
    on a morning when the yew pyramids were white with cobwebs,
When you had grown into a thin tall young girl;
But I would go back with you to earlier memories
    by night-light,
As it had been when other generations had their nurseries there,
    a hundred years before,
For we lived by candle and night-light without electricity.

A haunted room,
    surely, if ever room was haunted,
That night-nursery, though I believe not in ghosts;
Where a dead hand,
    had scratched with a diamond,
'*Charme des yeux à Renishaw*' upon the windowpane,

21

So all had not been melancholy,
    but it was a darkness out of which much came,
If engendered in melancholy in the big old house,
Where I remember listening in the dark, unable to fall asleep.

It so upsets me that you should be back there in your sleep
    in that primal darkness.
How pitiful it is!
While that other?
    It would have broken my heart when I was twelve years old
To see him sitting in the corner of his bedroom,
    as he sat here after his operation,
As he always sits now.

What else is there for him to do?
It is difficult to hear him when he speaks.
    He is half into that dark, too,
But clutching at the light,
The darkness at back and the dark in front of him,
    and of us all;
The two darks nodding, nodding to each other,
    and drawing nearer.
Ah! what can I say about it all!
    What sad, strange memories!

'His blood colours my cheek'

(on my sister dying)

'His blood colours my cheek'
Ah! but when that blood is no longer there;
I saw that, I saw that,
When the live thing had just gone,
    was those few moments gone,
Gone where,
    where, where?

Her open mouth,
When she was dead,
Her poor blanched cheek and forehead,
    and her pale hair,

As the turning off of a light?
As the snuffing of a candle,
    but the wick still glows
Till the smoke lifts?
      Even the smoke goes.

I wonder. And I fear:
As the falling star of light,
    and meteor,
Drops and extinguishes,
Falls faster than the falling tear

But not in her dying soul,
    which is all that matters,
Which is what is gone,
Which is where there was that promise

So she was not dismayed:
'His Blood coloured my cheek,'
    'I rise
To look in the compassionate,
    the all-seeing Eyes.'

Serenade to a Sister

You, my sister, have just gone away,
For whom, and whom only, I wrote poetry,
When young I was to net the Leonids,
But the world is not as I would have it be,
Nor you, nor I;
You, my sister, my soul of poetry,
No longer the young lioness,
Have just left and gone away,
Young lioness no longer,
The world is not as we would have it be,
Not you, nor I.

Now listen to the serenade:
'*Cortese damigella*',
Which means 'Gentle lady';
'*Donna non vidi mai simile a questa*',

23

'Never have I seen your like or equal';
'A dirle: io t'amo, a nuova vita
L'alma mia si destra,'
'To tell you I love you, wakens my soul to new life';
How beautiful and gentle the Italian!
But where will our souls go,
And shall we meet again?

'Come queste parole profumate
      mi vagan nello spirito mio,'
'How those scented words wander in my spirit';
'e ascosse fibre vanno a carezzare',
'And touch my heartstrings',
(And caress my quivering heartstrings would be
      a more literal translation)
'O susurro gentil . . . deh! non cessar, deh! non cessar!'
      (In the high notes of the tenor)
'May the gentle whisper of your words
Never cease,
May it go on for ever in the other world!'

There,
Lion and lioness shall have new coats,
And commune not with angels
But musicians,
Bright spirits will be poets, pianists,
All will be young and brilliant again;
But my paradise is not as yours,
You, my sister, would be bored with architects,
Buildings mean little or nothing to you,
You do not even look at them;
And yet the winds will be the brushing of a seraph's wing
In Venetian moonlight gliding or floating,
On August night,
When the lagoon waters are like aquamarine;
(Aquamarines
For you, my sister, to wear upon your hands).

I remember, also,
How long ago!
When the sun was setting,
You liked to look from the mirador
Of the Alhambra,
Across the river gorge to the Albaicín;
To music half-heard
Of guitar,

In the doorways of their caves,
Gypsies were dancing
In moon-dotted crinolines
You were there,
And not there at all,
As it could be Debussy
Writing of Granada where he had never been.

You love, I know,
The pergola of blue wisteria,
Below the lily-tower
And the little room
Where I am painted in fresco as a harlequin,
The hanging garden and blue paulownia tree;
But you will not walk there,
     'a cloister awaits me';*
And my answer; *'O gentile, qual fato*
     vi fa guerra?'
'What fate makes war upon you?'
Gentle nun, *'O gentile,'*
Your poetry is your nunnery,
Now nun, indeed, but warrior as well;
'Il mio fato si chiama',
'My fate calls and beckons to me'.

And for a strophe
Which I would not have you see;
'La mia stella tramonta,'
'My star is setting':
But my sister that shall not be:
'No! sul vostro destino riluce un altra stella',
I need not translate it:
'O susurro gentil . . . deh! non cessar, deh! non cessar!'

Will that be
A world as we would have it be,
My sister;
Or, once more, too late,
A fêting in oblivion,
As the Ancients in Etruscan tomb-mounds
Who recline in effigy on their coffins,
Pledging each other in eternal darkness;
Once in a hundred years,

---

* Written when I feared she would be hospitalized towards the end of her life.

25

Not more often,
An amphora rings a low note,
And every summer
In the tomb they hear the thunderstorm;
Does the bee come looking
Where is no nectar,
Only the buzzing of its wings could be the
  trumpets of *Fidelio*
Too late, too late.
Sister of my flesh and blood,
No more will happen.

You will be where I cannot get at you,
As to one part of your soul or spirit,
Where I cannot follow you,
Now abbess, but once,
'*Cortese damigella*',
As when I remember you, a young girl,
Vowed to poetry:
And yet I wonder:
It seems to me the substant,
Become transubstantial,
Brings little difference in immortality;
Your poetry, once you are dead,
Will be the second blooming of the rose;
In person you were the ghost of your own poems,
Haunting them, not to be removed from them,
And it is an easy transference to inhabit them entirely,
Once more a rose upon its own roots,
Not grown from the graft which was your mortal body.

Where are you refuged, my sister,
Among orisons and litanies?
The telling of the rosary
Is but a counting of the petals,
Is but a rose held in an old and withered hand,
Not hands as yours,
Supple and youthful,
That are the tiger in the tiger-lily.
You loved the heat! Come out into the sun!
I am lost in the dark wood,
The darkening wood that lies between,
This wood at edge of
The aphrodisiac beanfield,
Where dwell the horned owl and the nightingale.

Not lost in it,
So much as hiding here,
Rather as the suicide
Who only wants to be posted 'missing',
And found alive again,
Meanwhile, looking about me and listening,
As ever,
But the horned bird blinks or shuts its eyes;
So much for wisdom,
Which is blind in daytime and only sees at dark,
And as for the nightingale,
It sings with the orchestra
At full moon,
Or in the rose-bush a few feet from the trolley-buses
Of Tehran.

There is no bribing,
Or cajoling it to sing,
My sister,
And abbess of the nightingales,
Who wound up the clockwork in my mortal frame;
It sings, or sings not, on the Aventine,
And below the vineyard in the sacred wood
Where I walked when young, and heard it practising,
Scale upon scale as in a music school;
It has sung in me, and sung not,
Now it sings again.

I saw a phoenix on a factory chimney,
In the fading light,
Before the sun died in this sombre wood,
And a goddess wandering in the sweet-smelling field
Upon a morning
When every tree-trunk was the Venus of the isles;
The outskirts of every town was a fairground,
Apple and pear-trees in blossom
Were the star-clusters or nebulae,
Archipelagos of poetry,
For the Milky Way meandered through the orchard;
Or were they damson or cherry trees?
I scarcely knew.

That was my first beginning,
And you prompted it,

My sister;
Were ever such hands as yours for poetry?
To live as a young man in your flowering shade
Was wonderful indeed,
You could read a poem, and inspire one to poetry
By the inflections in your voice,
So that one went out, and the street musician
Was a starving genius,
The barrel-organ with tongue of metal,
Turning, churning in the rain,
Became all London in a hot sun,
Burning.

I can remember the tunes it played,
And singing them to myself,
Behold you again, my sister,
In your pelisse of green sheepskin
And wide brimm'd hat,
Standing by the statues
Where the walk goes down into the wood,
But you would not come more than a foot or two into the
    bluebells;
I suppose they are in bloom again at this moment,
In this month of June,
Just as the sun rose when we were a day old,
And will rise again the day after we are dead:
You would not walk, I say, into the bluebell wood.

I remember even the shape of the trees
In the lost paradise,
But they do not remember me;
A mist of the spirit hides him who stood between us,
There has been a spoiling and tainting of the honeyladen air,
For it was such while all three of us were young
And despite our troubles there was eternal spring;
Now it grows late,
And the black cloud makes darker still.

How bitter a dichotomy haunts you,
My sister,
Divides and haunts you,
Feeding on poetry from the earth's rough maws,
With hands like a lily but a lion's paws,
Compendium of rage and pity;
Of this world, but not of this world,

28

Refuged, and yet still in prison,
With no escape,
And that other, we both loved, in the prison with you,
The one a prisoner of the soul,
And the other imprisoned in and by his body,
Without hope of heart or mind to break his fetters,
Which are your manacles,
Just as though chained to the wall,
Though your dungeon alters from country house to castle,
But you keep indoors at both, and never go out into the garden.

I see you trailing in your long dress,
Like your own ghost, my sister,
For it is the shade of yourself that you projected and intended;
How poignant when I think back through,
They seem long summers of rain,
To when you would walk,
To where one never thought you could walk to,
In the Eckington woods round the lake,
I have been with you even as far as Cornelian Bay;
A long way indeed,
It seemed to the far side of the world,
At a time when you played the piano and were practising
    a *Romance* by Brahms,
You were perhaps twenty years old and had not begun to write
    poems,
It was before your poetry had become stronger than yourself;
The music, which I do not really like,
Reminds me of the hot blue bay,
But, also, our spirits are imprisoned in it
    as if they cannot get away,
For ever climbing on those rock pools
When the tide is out.

It haunts and saddens me,
There are indeed sad things to think of,
In this dichotomy, this divided world,
But I hear the strumming of the serenade,
My sister,
Your soul or psyche is here
With eyes closed but no! no! not sleeping.
We will not hear your window thrown open wide

To listen,
The curtain will be drawn, the window will be shut,

You work by intuition and by sensory perception
Upon, as it were, a limited keyboard,
But it is as the clavichord upon which can be played
    all the keyboard works of Johann Sebastian Bach,
There is nothing of feminine weakness about it,
It even gains in sensitivity from being played by feminine hands.

Ah! if only poetry were a universal language,
As has happened with music,
You would be as beloved as Chopin,
With whom there is the same fusion of the music and the
    person,
The one inseparable from the other;
But how many poets are hidden in their language,
Poets of the green tiles and the honeycomb
        in their love-songs,
            and
Gongora in the golden plateresco;
And now, *'Cortese damigella'*,
For the serenade addresses you in the Italian,
The tongue of the bravo and the Isola Bella,
'Donna non vidi mai simile a questa',
Your ghost will not come again, my sister,
Those who have not known you will wonder at you,
And there will come a day
When no one living remembers you,
I am thinking of that, and would tell them:

I knew her when she read poetry all day long
And was caught up on the wings of it,
Doomed to it,
As much as any aircraftsman standing too near to the propeller,
Who is drawn into the vortex
And the whirlwind;
In her person she was as Paolo and Francesca
Reading together in the light of the window,
And the sudden feeling comes over them,
And they are no more as others,
Fated together,
Drawn up into the great winds of feeling
Which bring suffering,
But laughter, also, and the rose and lily;
Poems of high spirit,
In youthful enjoyment and intoxication of technique,
As the encore pieces of a pianist,

Rose castles and waltzes, but even they are haunted,
In them, girl dances not with girl
As in the dance hall,
But it is the spectre waltzing with the rose.

I cannot be certain of my first memory of you,
It was perhaps when you were fourteen years old
In your not happy—more than unhappy childhood,
With every chance loaded against your becoming what you
    wished to be;
Already, even then, you were determined
Though drawn aside later into music
Till you were ready for it;

On the fourth floor, high in air,
How can I forget you opening the door
Like a statue from Chartres Cathedral,
Tall and thin:
Or on the long afternoons
Walking by the lake
To sound of near colliery and railway engine?
I have met your shadow
Down the lime avenue,
Long, long ago.

'Donna non vidi mai',
The ghost of you will not come again;
I have known no one so imprisoned in poetry,
As if besieged, embattled there;
But is the bee imprisoned in the foxglove,
Or the Red Admiral upon the buddleia?
What causes the honeygatherer
To creep back again and again into the rose;
They are not as workers driven down into the mines?

'Un chiostro m'attende' . . .
Are your words in the play;
'Domani all'alba io parto',
'I go away at dawn tomorrow,
'Soave fanciulla' of the serenade;
To have known and loved you,
And been your pupil and your brother
Is all I want of fame:
'O susurro gentil . . . deh! non cessar, deh! non cessar!'

The Golden City

Opus Anglicanum

We read of 'the late Mr Jack Elms
    cricket professional to the Sheffield United Club at Bramhall Lane
From 1880 until 1940.
Who each day during June and July
    would arrive on the ground
With a carnation of exhibition quality in his buttonhole,
    and never twice wore the same variety during any one summer'.

He was one of the last growers
    of pinks and carnations at Pitsmoor, outside Sheffield,
And 'Jack's carnations' were famous throughout the North;
His career we would call both the beginning
    and the end of things,
For it is at about the time that the whole country
    took to their oafish football and the Cup Final hysteria.

The harm had started a hundred years before
    when the shift of the rural workers into the towns had begun,
And the long rows of houses like the national disgrace of Arkwright
    Town,
    and the mining villages of Durham,
Brick kennels—and scarcely even that – with backyards of cobble
    stones,
Had replaced the cottages with their auricula frames
    of the silk-weavers of Lancashire,
And 'the gaudy tulip beds' even of the Mile End Road.

One does not have to be a Tolstoy,
    a Ruskin or a William Morris,
To see the horror and the wrong of this;
There is evidence in every direction if we only look for it
    of the wonders human beings have achieved
With perhaps a hundredth part of our present mechanical ability,
    who are now in this lifetime releasing ourselves from drudgery
And could be past masters both of the environment
    and of the lengthening hours of leisure.

What has been done for a small population
    could be done as well, or better, for a big one,
What is the matter with the planners?
    Have they seen nothing? Heard nothing?
Where have they spent their holidays?

Simple things, probably even the simplest things,
    must be the secret;
To have been the florist who found the first blue pansy,
    a chance seedling discovered among some heathers,
'Like a cat's face gazing up at me',
Rather than, in the same world of 'the fancy',
    like a former vicar of Church Langton in Leicestershire,
To have had more than a thousand varieties of gold-laced polyanthus,
Even were 'the yellow of true colouring,
    and as if the centre and petal edges had been treated with
  leaf-gold,'
And nearly the same number of auriculas growing in his garden;
For that was as though to be the autocrat
    who introduced conscription and compulsory military service
Among the 'improved' primroses and oxlips.

There was at least some warmth of proximity
    and of the human heartbeat
In the back-to-back kennels and outhouses of Arkwright Town,
Rather than in the shaking towers
    above the slag heaps and deserted pits
On the skyline of Sheffield,
And against the sunset, now, of London
    as of all big cities in the world tonight.

They need not have been,
    either the vertical, or the old-fashioned slum of slums,
Any more The Gorbals of Glasgow than the Hanging Gardens of
  Babylon,
And yet like our 'facts of life' and death,
    like Hitler and like Stalin,
They both are, and were, and both have been:—
    There was no necessity, and yet they had to be.

Rather the 'angel-ceilings' of East Anglian churches
    and their rookeries of wooden wings,
Than to live within earshot of an aerodrome
    and the wingless roar of 'jumbo' aeroplanes:—
So let us look about us and be comforted
    and see what was, and what could have been.

It is not needful to go far afield
        if the monastic barn of Great Coxwell be but an hour away,
Where the stone porch has a loft
        in which monks are said to have slept in harvest time,
When the 'nymph-hay' of Aubrey's phrase
        was scythed and garnered
From dewy fields of morn and early evening
        avoiding the heat of day,
Or the bales of wool counted
        under the smokeless sky.

The monk-builders, if required to do so,
        would have 'made something' of a gasometer or a power-station,
For there is nothing of intrinsic difference
        between a place for storage and a sewage-farm,
And if a barn can be turned into a temple of Ceres,
        the goddess of corn and of harvests:—
And such are the monastic barns of the West of England:—
Where artificial light is generated in order to dispel darkness
        could become the meeting place of the morning and the
                evening star.

I have no specific reason for mentioning Great Coxwell,
        except that nearly everywhere in England
There is something as quietly, unsensationally beautiful within a few
    miles;
        as the 'Marshland churches' between King's Lynn and Spalding
Which we still have to ourselves for no foreigner has heard of them;
Or the 'wool churches' of Long Melford and Lavenham,
        extraordinary for their length and number of windows,
Their porches and parapets of flushwork,
        or, in fact, mosaic of many-coloured flints.

Or the masterpiece which is the church at Heckington,
        the marvellous reticulation of its buttresses
With their receding planes and edges,
        the beautiful crocketing,
The delicate tracery of its seven-light east window;
Or, again, Patrington church,
        far out upon the banks of Humber,
With lantern tower, a tapering octagon
        to landmark the waters,
And unspoiled, unmatched interior of two aisles of arches.

Or the wonders of the West of England,
    which are many,
Not least in Tewkesbury,
Where the kneeling, mailed figure of a knight
    faces the altar,
And one does not like to speak,
    or make the least sound to mar his orisons.

But, mostly, it is the glory of the Perpendicular towers
    the like of which are only found here in this country;
Mere 'wool churches', but they have towers
That are as grandstands to listen to the music of the bells
    and look out over the sheepfolds and the rolling downs,
Through all the west and down to Somerset
    where they come to their end in galaxy,
And a lazy lifetime could be gone too quickly
    in looking and comparing them each to each.

Wooden rood-screens traversing both aisles and nave,
    reaching right across the church
At Bradninch and Dunchideock in Devon,
    like one hedgerow only of a pilgrim's way,
Or Green Lane in full summer flowering
Of dog-roses, or wild Gypsy roses we could call them,
    near to some limp rags,
A pair of old boots and the ashes of a bonfire,
In prophecy of 'travellers' not yet come ashore;
    elder blossom, honeysuckle, blackberries they could be,
And for full measure 'fairy' apples
    of deadly nightshade,
In epitome of high summer all in the carving.

There must be amateurs of the rose-window,
    blue roses of the rosomane from the larger churches,
But our counterpart to honeycomb and stalactite
    of the Moors of 'El Andaluz';
To the swan-domes of the Mughals
Which are of white peacock, lily, swan analogy;
    or to the blue vaults of Isfahan,
Is the fan-vault ceiling,

As of the palm-tree recently clipped and trimmed
    for some two-thirds of its circumference,
And the palm-fronds trained into concentric circles;

Or like a bunch of parachutes descending with their segments
    touching;
        or, again, open umbrellas but held upside down
To shake off a shower;
Or, fourthly, like spinning tops or gyroscopes,
        the complete circle seen, and as it were, set in motion
By a hemicycle on the wall that touches it,
        to keep it spinning,
As in the Henry VII Chapel at Westminster.

Such are wonders that exist nowhere else
        and are an important part of our patrimony,
It is too late now to grow auriculas,
        there is too much smoke pollution and too little patience;
But, in retrospect, such and their like are the last conscious effort
        to have a personal involvement with the world we live in,
Not to listen dumbly and let everything to chance,
        but to give direction and leave behind a mark,
Humble cousins, therefore, to the towers and spires
And of what their bells give warning:—
        that we live but once;
And the rest is dead music:
        dying, dying, dead.

Liselund

Where?
    Oh! Where?
And with whom alive or dead?
Now it is getting a little late to be writing *galantieren*,
        as I prefer to call them,
When I should be putting my affairs in order
        and trying to conjecture what comes next

Oh! to be starting off on a fine morning,
        as so often in the past,
To find something fresh and beautiful
        we had not known before!

We hear the horns of the hunt come nearer,
        and once more it is the cottage

'To one side of the stage',
Where Giselle the dark-eyed daughter
    lives with her mother under the mouse-fur thatch

The *cottage orné* of Liselund,
    on the Baltic isle of Møn,
Where are too the white chalk cliffs of Caspar David Friedrich:—
Liselund most lovely of all love nests,
    its only peer maybe
The Swiss Cottage in the green demesne of Cahir

Swiss Cottage of Cahir

Oh! the river that runs along
The smooth lawns of Cahir
Running like music through the green demesne,
Where deep flows the river and dark lies the shade

A rustic cottage, a *'cottage orné'*
Stands high and hanging woods behind,
Thatched roof, white walls
And antlered balconies
For hot noons; as now,
And also for moonlight and the Milky Way;
It has a room with little paintings from Canton
Of beauties as fragrant
As the gardenia or jessamine teas,
And a room with a landscape wallpaper:—

The thatch is as soft as moleskin,
Cut and sewn,
The hanging woods are a backcloth or a 'painted drop'

It is the meeting-place of the anglers:—
Does never a fisherman
Casting his line late in the evening
When the woods are unreal
And there is late light upon the mullions
When deep glides the river and the shades are long,
Cast again and again upon his pool

And catching the little rainbow trout
Flecked and spotted with vermilion
That dies and lies gasping,
Feel the magic and poetry of the enchanted hour
And know this is the maiden
Of the dancing waters,
The maiden of the river
And the ghost of the Swiss Cottage
In the green demesne of Cahir?

The Rose-Pink Chapel

'The single aisle (1756) painted rose-pink and decorated by Pedrozzi with stucco-work is a feast for the eyes.'   Guide Michelin

Two paintings by Caravaggio in Roman churches, sacristies in Spain and Italy, and more besides.

1

Yes! Indeed the Chapel is beautiful
    and does for the moment quite take one's breath away,
Remembering it this misty October morning
    with the mist just lifting,
Until in mid-afternoon
    we sit on a tree-stump in the autumn sunlight
Talking of the hi-jacked Lutfhansa now landed in North or South Yemen,
    with the eleven poor terrified beauty queens on board,
Which should tie down the day, almost the hour*

The Rose-pink Chapel being one of the beauties of the world
    in that age of music before the big orchestras had begun;
If no more so,
    than a rose-pink silk-taffeta coat,
A man's coat in an attic here,
Of ribbed silk with a *reflet* of green in the white ribs of it,
    and white lace waistcoat over the pure rose-pink satin;
At just the year of *Nozze di Figaro*, I am thinking,

* 18 October 1977. The trajectory of terror extended from Palma de Mallorca to Mogadishu in Somalia at the 'horn' of Africa.

For 'youth more glitt'ring than a Birth-Night Beau',
    Cherubino or no,
Who wore the rose-pink coat at Court

It being the sheer irreligiosity of the Rose-pink Chapel
    that is so captivating,
As in all things that bring,
    or could have brought condign punishment,
Or even a sentence of death for not believing in;
So that it is like treading on air or being given wings
    just to step within its precincts,
At how many million miles remove
    from all or any martyrologies

Forgive this once,
    the fires of Smithfield and of the Quemadero,
Burning-place of the Holy Office or Spanish Inquisition!
'Large deposits of ashes, cinders and human bones were found,'
    only as long ago as 1868,
And this in the middle of the modern city of Madrid:—
Convictus et combustus was the terse, laconic entry
    in their roll-call of the dead:—
Not that the Holy Office had the monopoly of burning,*
While the frozen tundra still kept hid its mammoth bones
    and the psychic ward for dissidents was as yet unheard of

So now again,
    to where the Rose-pink Chapel of the Margravine awaits us,†
And once more takes our breath away
    till one forgets all other themes,
Because it is what a possible, acceptable religion could have been,
    holding out no promises of immortality
In an overcrowded heaven

But only the immediacy of a moment
    and a memory to hold to,
For no longer I would say,
    Than the memory of a walk when young
    with mind full of poetry
Along the rose-hung hedges

---

* Note, also, in front of the basilica of the Sacré-Cœur at Montmartre, the statue of the Chevalier de la Barre, burned alive here in 1766 at the age of nineteen for impiety, i.e. for not taking off his hat as the 'host' was carried past. This, at the apogee of Louis Quinze furniture and gold snuff-boxes. The poor victim would have been only sixty-eight years old in 1815 at the fall of Napoleon.
† The Margravine Wilhelmine of Bayreuth was sister to Frederick the Great of Prussia.

And now we put fifty lire in the box
    and all the lights go on:—
Where else the Saint with outstretched arms,
    a statue robed in lapis,
In lapis lazuli,
    but at the Roman church of Il Gesù?

It is the altar of St Ignatius
    by 'Fratel' Pozzo* and 'assistants',
For he had his troupe or team who worked with him,
Perspectivist,
    master of the arts of *quadratura* and *sotto in su*.

No one man lying on his back on a scaffolding
    a few inches below the ceiling,
To which he had to climb wearily each morning
    and come down at nightfall,
Could have painted the entire vault and dome
    of the other Roman Jesuit church of Sant' Ignazio:—
All in order that the figures and the painted architecture
    should be seen in correct perspective
From a round marble floor-slab in the centre of the nave,
    a feat of near-maniacal complexity and uselessness.

After dislike of which,
    it is a return almost to sanity
To come out and admire the little piazza
In front of Sant' Ignazio built like the drop-scene
    and side-wings of a theatre.

To which category, but it is sacred
    and not secular,
Belongs this altar to Sant' Ignazio in the church of Il Gesù,
    with a lighting 'Fratel' Pozzo can never have dreamt of;
The bronze candelabra, the bronze altar-railings
    in their convolutions,
All being accessory to that extraordinary moment
    when the lights go on

The pairs of altar-columns all inlaid
    as though 'filletted' with lapis,

* Andrea Pozzo, a native of Trentino, 1642–1709.

The Saint in embroidered dalmatic of lapis lazuli,
The niche in which he stands, even the half-dome above his head
    all inlaid with lapis,
Out of which the life goes
     when the lights turn off

The House of the Presbyter

To Geoffrey Elborn for his support and friendship

1

Sometimes,
    not often enough,
Just as I fall asleep:—
Coming to a whitewash'd wall,
    climbing a hilly street,
I am at the House of the Presbyter
    in the huge old fig-tree's shade

All is white as snow within his house,
    where the women walk on chopines or pattens
Like those of Aretino's courtesans
    on the Venetian bridges,
And have henna'd fingertips;
Their chintz dresses are sprigg'd with flowers,
    and they wear bandanna'd turbans
And earrings of gold and coral from the isles

But the old priest leads us to his pigeon-lofts,
    where the shadows of the fig-tree are blue upon the walls,
And one by one he takes a bird upon his wrist,
    or beckons them to come to him from boughs and cages;
What a flurry of their fan-shaped tails
    spread open to show the markings;
They flutter and come down, they hover and fly up again,
    their wings are never still!

We see their round eyes in their milk-white heads,
    white feathers or bootees to their feet,
And milky chests all frilled and ruffed;

41

Their heads are shell-crested
　　like a little hood or peak;
Some are grouse-legg'd
　　and others arrow-tipp'd upon their shoulders

And now they come flurrying down in all their colours,
　　dark-headed with laced shoulders,
Of every shade, red, yellow, brown, or sulphur,
　　black or dun, as well as blue or silver,
Listen! Oh! listen
　　It is Dodona in a little house,
Half-way up a little hill.

Satin, or spangled blondinettes,
　　bluettes, or silverettes,
That are satinettes with bars instead of lacing;
The blue-laced and the sulphur-laced
　　perhaps for predilection out of the satinettes,
Silly names! But who has thought of better?

It is the race of Oriental Frills,
　　and it could be that this whole family
Are the most beautiful of all pigeons,
　　traced by Mr Caridia their discoverer*
To the House of the Greek Presbyter in Smyrna
　　and having a history of two hundred years or more,
For the Presbyter said they were bred and propagated
　　by his father and grandfather before him;
Or, in fact, bluettes, satinettes and blondinettes
　　to take the place
Of Turks and Greeks and Levantines

2

But we would assay the atmosphere of old Smyrna:—
　　Here are to be seen and heard,
The French with a dialect and strange mode of spelling;
　　the High Dutch, i.e. Hollanders, an old colony but speaking
　English;
Opium is chiefly in the hands of the Hollanders,
　　and sent to Java:—for the batik'd rajahs,
Their gamelan orchestras to inspire them,
　　their bayadères of the tilted eyes
And long gilded fingernails

* Mr H. P. Caridia was a Greek from Smyrna who settled in Birmingham, then the centre
of the pigeon-fancy, in the eighteen-sixties.

Other products of old Smyrna:
    liquorice paste,
Unrefined, obtainable from Messrs McAndrew and Forbes;
Sponges reach the value of a quarter of a million piastres;
    Attar-of-roses is an article of export;
Likewise scammony—what is scammony?—
    still a large article of trade;
And galls, but yellow berries have fallen off;
The leech business, formerly very good,
    and for which there are large tanks, has fallen off

And amenities;
    camel fights are now very rare
A favourite picnic ground is near the grotto of the Seven
    Sleepers;
In the High Turkish quarter is a tekeh
    of the Whirling Dervishes;
Zebeck dancing must be seen in distant villages,
    where occasionally Turkish mountain music may be
    heard,—
Nomads may be seen along the two railways,
    and to the right and to the left a great Gypsy camp;
And we have an idea of life in Smyrna

But not of the luxury of quiet,
    the clarity and stillness
In this Levant of Liotard;
The Presbyter is eighty years old and more,
    and whether or not Phanariot,
I do not know;
Or if he has seen the Greek isles,
    and the flat-roof'd houses of the Cyclades

There are so many things I want to ask him;
    but just as I am about to question him
Something happens,
    and I am awake again

3

I try once more,
    a night or two later,
As a fat negress passes by, unveiled,
    under the fig-tree,
In wide yellow trousers;

And lo and behold! I am at the House of the Presbyter again.
    Listen! Oh listen!
Once more it is Dodona in a little house,
    half-way up a little hill

And we are talking,
    not of the domes like kettledrums of the Janissaries
Menacing the skyline of Istanbul,
But of the tiled mosques with inners walls of china,
    Sokollu Mehmet Pacha and Rustem Pacha,
Buildings,
    that soothe and calm as does no other architecture

Pulpits or *minbars* quite spired with tiles,
    patterned with flowering trees,
Their stems wreathed with lilies, tulips and carnations;
Smaller mosques with tiles of vases
    holding sprays of blue fruit-blossom at Atik Validé;
Panels of red currants, all luscious and gleaming at Ibrahim
  Agha;
And red borders the results of liquefied coral
    in the mosque of Ramazan Effendi:—
The names themselves being a strong suit of the magic

All in keeping
    with the perfection of his pigeons,
Their cooing and preening
    and the volleying of their wings:—
There are so many things I want to ask him
    about his pigeons

And how much he knows about the Ancients?
    Has he seen the empty theatre, not far away,
Where the figure of a female in the centre of the colonnade
    springs from the calyx of a flower,
Holding branches of foliage in her hand?
For that is more serious than all the Turkish nonsense

But, again,
    Just as I am about to question him,
Something happens,
    and I am awake again

La Sueña

Oh! it is so hot, so hot,
In this land of whitewashed walls,
Of the blue gulf and the Turkish fishing town;
This land of jasmine and of orange blossom,
Hammamet, where jasmine is held in every hand,
Where the clustered jasmine lies behind the ear,
Where the sands have stranded porpoises and flying-fish,
And tortoise and chameleon hide in the agave,
In the armoured agave bristling with its points.

Listen! oh! listen to the lapping of the waves,
Most loud at the Kasbah, at the castle wall,
Of snow-white ramparts, where the trumpet sounds
To cohort of Niger and of Senegal,
Dark as porphyry, darker than basalt,
Posted in the barracoon,
Here it was, in sight of this, that long dead things
Whispered their words,
In the pitiful silence, in the dead hour before dawn;
The dancer danced again, and stayed awhile
By the pearlshell window opening on the day,
And spoke in her solemn voice, and wept in sweetness.

Then wonder of wonders, as never in a dream,
The pearlshell hour, the first breath of the morning,
Brought her again to me,
And we wept together at the cooling of our hearts,
Though mine it was that smouldered, for her heart was never
    mine,
Though I held it in my hands and blew on it to fan its flame,
But we wept to be parted,
In that sweet breath fragrance, in the dawning of the day,
For then my youth left me and I turned towards the snows,
I woke up weeping, and reached out for the jasmine,
For the bunch of jasmine lying by my hand;
She died in that sweetness; we both died together,
Like lovers who are dead from it, and drop to sleep,
To dreamless sleep,
So died the jasmine; and it was scentless.

Chichecastenango

Here
     I saw
What I had not seen before
A carpet of pine-needles
Green pine-needles
     on the floor
New strewn
     that morning
Smelling
     fresh and sweet
Soften than sawdust
     to the feet

Tribute to Taxco

Taxco,
     when I was young,
Was three days ride on mule-back
Across the mountains of the state of Guerrero;
Now it is two hours from Mexico City
On a motor-road.

At Cuernavaca
We were given chirimoyas,
Grenadillas, sapotes,
Mangoes and papayas,
It was our first taste of the tropics:—
Warm nights like faded gardenias of Mexico,
And time to anticipate her golden churches.

Near a road sign
To Acapulco and the Pacific,
There were white flowering trees;
Acapulco port of galleons
From China and Manila,
And the 'plate fleet' from Peru.

And what is it now?
    Taxco has become like Greenwich Village;
    But there are still the flowers and half-dead volcanoes;
    And on the road to Taxco
    The white flowering trees.

Benin Bronze Head of a Girl

A girl's neck thin and round as a stalk
And her spoon-shaped, beautiful full-lipp'd Negress face,
        the true Negress with nothing of the Nilote,
And tall horn-like headdress
Curving like a rhinoceros horn,
        a net or snood of coral
Coming forward over her eyes,
A bronze head, only a bronze head,
        no body or limbs,
But a princess of Benin of the fifteenth century

So they had sculptors and casters of bronze all that time ago.
And where had they learnt? In Portugal?
        But there is nothing of the kind in Portugal.
It was an African who renewed the arts of Egypt
In this only greatness of Africa,
        being pagan not Moslem,
Pagans released in their generation from the witch-doctors and
            the juju-men

And all at once the murderous dawn,
Where violence has been done once already in the hut
        to this ghost with the slave-skin,
The young girl comes crawling on hands and knees

Through an opening no bigger than a dog's door in the wall,
        to stand up in the dark beside me,
With her body almost touching me,
Where were no legs or arms before,
And her neck flowers into her shoulders
Down her arms, her elbows and her thin, child's waist
        which spins round of itself if you but touch against it,

Being the stem of the same plant as her neck,
Though a bronze head and only a bronze head,
    with no limbs or body

And the light of dawn touches her coral headdress,
The curving horn or cornucopia of her headdress,
    and gleams on her shoulders as she gets down again,
Living body, spoon-shaped face,
    and young animal

Nigritian

Here,
    could be a golden age for a lifetime,
But for no longer
Of all the Negro races become republics,
    only in Nigeria, and nowhere else.
For the Negro cannot maintain it,
And after a generation always it dies down
    and falls in bloodshed;
But there could be a condominium of Pagan and Moslem,
As of another 'Stupor Mundi' Hohenstaufen,
    republic certainly no longer then,
And only little different from tyranny.
Where else in Africa could there be sculptors?
For there will be great sculptors,
    this is in the Negro genius,
Where else is there this school of life
That lends itself to abstraction;
And music,
    talking-drums that imitate the tone sounds of Yoruba words,
And speak, syllable by syllable, across the cotton-fields,
    over the ground-nut groves,
With fiercer preludings or fanfares
Taken from the flourishes of the caboceers;
    A land where the women are dressed in all shades of blue,
With indigo-dyed turbans,
A time when it is worth while to be alive.

The Microcephaloid of Dakar

That day, and the next day,
    and never again
The microcephaloid;
Although we looked for him
    all through the market-place;
Less than five feet tall,
    with his begging bowl,
A long staff in his other hand

His stained, white burnouse;
    and now his face:—
The spider-bitten bags beneath his eyes,
Mouth, with lips just like the eye-bags,
    and sparse tuft of beard;
Eyes that are hardly open,
    or have not begun to see;
The sleep of the dead fish,
    and the new born monster-child

His skull:—
    six to eight inches high,
With a knitted cap round the peak of it
To make it higher, thinner still,
    where it was no bigger than a two-shilling piece:
Dark-skinned,
    not Negroid of feature,
More like a sage from the Diamond Mountains of Korea
    to my eyes

Who knitted his cap for him?
    Who sent him out to beg upon the streets,
This beggar who was like a being
    from a fairy story?

Not Negroid, or African in the least,
But an anchorite from among the Moutan paeonies,
    begging in the market-place in Senegal
Among a populace of porphyry and anthracite

Where the dresses of the Negresses
    are more beautiful than anywhere in Africa;
Negresses with straight noses
    and smooth shoulders;
Not patterned cottons of Ghana and Nigeria,
    made in Manchester,
But dresses of the cheapest and the gayest nylon stuffs,
Shot with gold and silver
    for their baggy pantaloons,
And the hand of Schéhérazadé
    to arrange and fold their turbans

The King of Morocco was on a state visit,
    the Negresses were wearing their best dresses;
There were elderly matrons with the mien of Roman
    Empresses,
With their maids walking a pace or two behind them,
        and no one looking at the beggar-anchorite with the high
    pointed skull
Around whom a whole cycle of stories could be written,
    Why did we lose him in the crowd?
Why could we never see him again?

There was the giant night-porter of the hotel N'Gor,
    all in blood-red like an executioner,
When we touched down from Recife in South America at
    4 a.m.,
And at that other dawn out in the cold air,
    Sitting on a three-legg'd stool at the hotel door,
Looking out over Africa with his hands upon his knees,
    both villain and hero of its miseries!
And where was the homunculus?
    Was he awake, or sleeping,
When we walked out into the morning,
    and climbed the skies?

Pineta

Pinewoods of the Tyrrhenian shore
With angel-youths galloping in the night-hunt
Through torchlit dark as in Uccello's painting;

Not forgetting in this Guatemalan pinewood
Alessio Baldovinetti's
Far off winding rivers and his trees,
Dying to nothing down the empty distances;
White stems of cypress along the Arno valley,
Stone pines with never wind in them,
Still as a fig tree in a wilderness;
And Pisan pinewoods of Benozzo
Down the long littoral to the Claudian ilex,
To the volcano's stone pine or smoke
And siren shore.

The Shrines of Ise

It began to pour with rain
As we walked under the cryptomerias
Thunder shook and rattled
The white cocks and hens had run for safety,
Ah! the solemn and enormous tree-stems
At the Shrines of Ise
Each taller than a ship's mast
And touching the rain clouds,
To the turn in the path where the trees were taller still,
And now it is deluging down and becoming frightening,
One is wet through, with water running from one's face and
    hands.

The wet smell of the pine forest is living and animal
Now we come to low Maori-looking huts,
And can see the golden roof of the forbidden shrine
Built in another clearing in the forest every twenty years
Of new, unvarnished cedar of the finest grain;
And go on through the downpour to the *Kagura-den*,
Or sacred dancing hall
Where the maidens of the god,
Virgin-priestesses,
Dance for us in scarlet divided skirts
With pine-trees painted on their fans;
On their heads a tiara of coral,
A little branching tree of coral
On their sleek black hair,

And in their other hand a green wand,
A green wand of the sacred *sakaki* tree;
Their dance is a lustration
A purification ceremony;
And the Shinto priest in a white robe,
With the hilt of his sword showing,
Has a black, ant-like headdress,
A headdress like the whole outline of an ant,
With a spray of some yellow flower
Tucked into his black hat at its waistband,
And holds a sceptre of dark wood in his hand

Swinging Festival of the Brahmins

'About the middle of March the Hindus observe a swinging festival in honour of the god Khrishna, of whom a doll or image about three feet high is placed in the seat or cradle of a swing, and just as the dawn is breaking, rocked gently to and fro.'

H. G. Quaritch Wales, *in* Siamese State Ceremonies, *1931*

Beyond the white walls and dragon-roofs of Wat Prajohit,
     in the 'city centre' of the Sharawaggi Kingdom,
Where the temples arc of sherds of glass and broken china,
     the dragon-barges lie in their boathouse
And the white (albino) elephant is in his stable,
I have seen the pillars of the giant swing,
     all a-glitter in the paradisal light of morning,
Eighty foot high like ships' masts painted red,
     hauled by elephants,
Then floated down out of the teak forest

The festival is the yearly arrival of the god on earth,
     in pantomime,
Played by a temporary king who impersonates him
     in robes subtly differenced from those of the real king,
And wearing a tall pointed magician's hat;
     with him are acrobats and persons dressed as 'sprites
     from celestial spheres',
The teams of swingers wear naga-headdresses
     like the hoods of serpents,

The game being to catch with the teeth
        a purse hanging from a bamboo pole;
They make many feints at it in order to amuse the crowd,
At each success gongs are beaten, conches blown;
        when the ceremony ends,
The naga-swingers dance round the swing
        and throw water over each other from buffalo horns,
It is clearly a solar ceremony of Ancient Indian origin.

So let the Brahmins put up their pairs of posts
        and rock to and fro their images of the god,
They have long forgotten it is a solar ceremony;—
        yet in the *Rigveda* the sun is called 'the golden swing in
    the sky'.
And to take it to its origins;—
        if it be the swing of Khrishna,
Who,
        the swinger?
There need be but one
        to start him off and catch him back again
From Himalaya to Himalaya,
        the snowy pillars of his giant swing,
Down and across hot India from end to end.

One might wonder who is in the swing,
        who is in the swing with him
As he rides across the sky?
For Khrishna was no solitary;—
        his inseparable companions
Were the sacred milkmaids or *gopis*,
Devidases, apsarases,
        call them what you will!

There will have been more than one *gopi*
        to keep him company,
With the huge earrings and long necklaces
        of temple dancers,
Each,
        with her channel of spine
That leads to her shoulder,
        as with the stone maidens of Khajuraho,
And the heavy chignon upon her scented neck

Or
        (for it is insidious)

53

A swing for amorous dallying
    as the August nightfall deepens
In the lime avenues of Le Nôtre;
And his already centenarian top-sails
    and top-gallants
In line ahead,
    still dropping sweetness,
Hang idle in the doldrum evening;
But this is no fête galante
    in Bourbon hunting woods round Paris;
No splashing fountains and no orangeries;
Nor cedarn beams, nor Andalusian apiaries,
    no swans'-down domes,
Nor floating voices from the minarets.

Khrishna's
    was a paradise of prolix ornament,
Of monkey-slums
    and flying-foxes
Sleeping head-downwards from the trees.

And what does Khrishna see up there?
    What does he pass by in the sky?
With the moon no more than a handmirror,
    a mirror with a dead face in it?
Does he sight maned suns,
    the lion-dawns of distant mornings;
Parhelions in galaxy,
    wandering tribes that light their tinker-fires at nightfall
On uncharted evenings?

Or the grander interludes and processions,
    timed circus-entrances we would call them,
All spangles and glittering sky-chariots,
    rehearsed and played how many evenings
In the giant tent of the night skies?

But Khrishna,
    'the lovely youth of Ganges in a yellow robe,'
Alighting from the heavens,
    setting foot on earth again,
A living god stepping from a palanquin,
Has seen nothing, heard nothing,
    and is interested only in his *gopinis*
And his own pipe-playing.

Dionysia

1

In the steaming incense
    oxen-breath of thousands
In aching cold
    that hurts the fingernails
The falling snow the only gentleness

The church of the onion-domes
    and holy idiots
'Idiotic for Christ's sake'
Even the chains and iron cap
    worn by one of them for penance

The waxen, yellowing mummy
    in its glass case
Facing the faceless men in cloth caps
    upon the rostrum

A clanking, rumbling of tanks
    ever bigger and uglier
Than the chains of all the convicts
    who ever started on the long march
From prison to Siberia

Or Hannibal's war elephants
    born again in cast-iron
With treads to obliterate on and on
    into the mind

Or scorching fire from their nostrils
    if so minded
While overhead in the fog and snow
    cetaceans of the louds

55

Sharks that can do everything
          but turn sideways upon their backs
And bite
          pass so low we bow our heads in fear

But now the sensation
          of this year's parade
There appears a truck
          a thirty-two-wheeled truck
Scurrying like a centipede across the square

Supporting
          a gross and fearful parody
Of the human instrument and weapon
          of procreation

With intent to rape
          and burst the calyx
And wobble the earth upon its axis;
Their best,
          this far,
Show of rocketry

And after?
          Where is anything? It is all gone.
Alike, Wall Street and the London Stock Exchange
          alike, Las Vegas and El Alamo,
The Pyramid of Kheops
          and the skyscrapers down Fifth Avenue;
Alike, everything that is,
          or ever was,
And everything there will ever be;
Not a soul left on the airports or the subways,
          no one living in the Polaris submarines;
Red Square all gone,
          and St Peter's and the Parthenon

And so to their fireless flats:—
          with not a laugh or smile
Upon a human face

Temple of Khajuraho

It is the night of the ritual orgy
The ranks of *devidases,*
    apsarases, mandanakas
Call them what you will!
Stand one above another,
    three rows of them,
On buttresses that are as clustered organ-pipes
    upon the organ-towers of Khajuraho

Temples
    that are of vegetable growth,
Like ribboned corncobs in ridges of little segments;
Or like opuntia cactus,
    but hairless and without the spines;
They have not the white cactus-wool
    that is as a caterpillar's covering or clothing;
But the main towers and side towers
    clustered together
Have the shapes of mountains with their scattered rocks;
And the eye ascends the lesser turrets,
    or *urusringas,*
Which are lesser mountains
On the flank of the world-mountain Meru;
And down again to the three bands
    of apsaras on the buttresses
Between the balconies or open porches

Maidens
    in the stone rigging
Who as though to shake the dew from them
    quiver their bodies alive:
A shoal of maidens caught in the stone rigging
Standing
    with each her pediment and cornice
    over and above her head
In every mesh or compartment
Up the stone rigging of Khajuraho:
But particularly at the corners
    where they stand out in profile;

And all around on the stone pedestals
        are satyr-priests, turban'd, bearded,
Each ready in his corner

Look up at the *apsarases*
        in high headdresses of flowers,
Apsarases
        who wear but mitres of jasmine in their bee-black hair
Which are the carvings?
        Which the living bodies?
For the sculptors had the school of life under their eyes
As much as Belsen or Dachau were the schools of death
Is not one kind of love,
        the profane,
As strong, or stronger than the other?
We see this nowhere else in the world but at these temples
        built in the same years as our abbeys and cathedrals

Some, the gods and their *apsarases*,
        on the spokes of the huge wheels,
As though whirling interlocked,
        and in the whirr of it held still
Down ten centuries;
But that is on the sun's chariot at Konarak
And we go back to the spires of Khajuraho
        to look up at the *apsaras*,
In fetichist-fingered high headdresses of flowers;
It is no longer love-making
        but a feast of cannibals,
Which is not for pale bodies and pale skins
Bhuvaneswar
        Konarak
                Khajuraho
Are in the tropics

And the orgy of the Kaulas
Is not as the loves of Khrishna
        and his *gopinis*
Who were the milkmaids of Himalaya;
Or the sacred fire and the intoxication
        in its beginnings,
Before the orgy knew not where to stop

3

Dionysia
(as told by Athenaeus, after Callixenes of Rhodes)

And now to the Dionysia
    on an early evening
In the time of Ptolemy II Philadelphus
At Alexandria, 'where the commodities of India are brought',
The Scanderoon of the Turks and the red-pied
    hawk-nosed pigeons,
Just when the statues of the gods begin to go past,
    tottering of step,
Put down every two minutes by their bearers,
    and no saetas from the balconies

Then, a long wait,
    and at last, one and then another,
The clashing cymbals of the Bassarids,
Spreading like sparks of fire through the crowd,
    like the dropping of a tray of iron
Hurled down upon the ground and ringing, ringing;
And yet once again,
    a shaking and banging the castanets
In the ears of Silenus and Casey;
Bird-clacking of the crotales
    which is like the clackclack
Clack from the prompter's box;
Or bamboo bird-clacking
    for the puppets of the Bunraku-za

The crowd are eating shellfish as at the bull-fight
    but, also, they suck pomegranates
Of Melegrana, the pomegranate garden;
While in his pavilion,
    a pavilion as luxurious as a summer palace,
The Pharaoh of the Hellenes
And Arsinoe, his sister-wife in Ptolemaic custom,
Sup on hyena-liver,
    the highest delicacy of the Old Egyptians

And the lynxes and the phrases in Greek script
    of Ezra the blacksmith,
Rämistrasse 29, a keos keeauvos, 'and carried away all his flocks
   and herds'

Kobori Enshu, Casey again, and all the rest of them?
Drowned, all drowned, when midday came,
  in the Tocado da Gloria,
The sound of the great bell of the Giralda,
'Indescribable in excitement, a clashing of cymbals
  as loud as thunder, or the roar of cannon.'

Now the ithyphalli are dancing in the crowd;
  and the phallus-bird from the kyathos in Berlin,
A girl astride a giant bird of wood and feathers
  which she works with both feet,
A bridle on the long neck of the bird is the phallus;
And behind her come the floats with tableaux vivants,
Of Leda coupling with her swan,
Shown on the handlamps of the Ancients
  to light them upstairs to bed;
Or it could be where are the swan-breeding grounds,
Among the reeds and water-meadows
  of Maeotis and Tanais;
Or Pelops and Hippodamia fleeing in a chariot
  through the gentian fields
To the pleasures that await them

All such, I read,
  'against a background of luxuriant vegetation,'
Before the lemon or the cactus came,
  but with the vine the pine
  the olive and the oleander,
With no more of glitter than the ilex shade;
As, for instance, Phaedra in a swing,
A gentlemanly satyr her cavalier or squire,
  who portends no harm to her,
Not as those satyrs who would throw themselves on running
    animals,
And should make up a landing party
  for the Isola dell' Asinara
To rut with the wild white asses
Upon the asphodel, acanthus, and dwarf-palmetto
  of the Sardinian mainland

It reads 'Indian triumph'
  on the handwritten posters,
And there are mock-saddhus smeared with ashes,
Trident in hand as on sentinel along the Ganges,

In acrid smoke from the burning ghats
    who rake the embers;
And *hierodoules* or *apsarases*,
Not of the race of Arsinoe or Cleopatra,
Still less,
    that of the gondolier's fair daughter
And painter's model,
Posed in Roman colonnades against a pyramid
As Queen of Egypt,
    but with white coursers,
    white clouds of the lagoon,
Far out from the city of the campanile,
Near where I saw pomegranates and fishing-nets of Malamocco.

And now to the climax of the Dionysia,
    as described by Athenaeus, after Callixenes of Rhodes,
Who tells of a chariot bearing a golden thyrsus,
    ninety cubits long,
A cubit being half-longer again than so many feet,
And therefore longer than any vehicle we meet upon the road
    with motor-cycle escort,
Mistaken for an important prisoner being moved from jail to jail
At utmost speed, but this other goes dead slow,
Blocking the traffic for mile in front and behind it;
    And a silver lance of sixty cubits,
Another emblem of Dionysus,
Lying on the same chariot beside it;
If you call 'a chariot' a float or car,
    drawn 'Indian fashion' by many hundreds of devotees.

And after it another chariot
With a gilded phallus a hundred and twenty cubits long,
Hung with golden streamers,
    and with a gold star six cubits in circumference at the end of it;
The phallophoroi walking to either side,
Their heads crowned with ivy and with violets;

'And others with white striped garments reaching to the ground,
    and on their hands they wear gloves composed of flowers';
Noble virgins carrying little golden baskets filled with fruits,
Walking beside the closed waggon or van of Bacchus
    which holds his mysteries;
A tracking-station, it could be, to direct
    the satellites in orbit,
Both a listening-post and the unlikely looking

Nerve centre,
        Master-mistress
Of the launching-pad;
And, indeed, directress of the battery-chickens,
Who directs them when and where they drop their eggs,
From and out of which spring giants and funguses of smoke,
        only and authentic way to split the womb of time,
And leave earth to the cockroaches
    ˙ where the mushroom cloud has finished.

But these are fructifying forces of the earth,
        not death,
For all the decadence of the Ptolemies of Egypt,
Aping the Pharaohs,
Thirty dynasties of those, and reigning for as many centuries,
Now enervated by the Macedonians,
        tired with India,
And lax from the plunder of Persepolis;
The Dionysia of the Greeks being no different in kind
        from he who would pray to the pear-tree on the wall,
Or walk with the Stone Age men of Malekula,
Essential goodness on narrow principles being no part of their
    religion,
        that being an end to itself
Among the distorted following of the 'pale Galilean',
Where the 'saints', so many of them, are the wrong sort of saints,
And the worship of the god in ourselves and of the forces in nature
        the only true religion.

Musicalia

Baraka ('as the Moors call it')

1

Or the recharging and refuelling
    of the human and mortal dynamo
'For the great work of influencing the next year's harvest,'
    According to person,
Which in this instance is the Virgén de Araceli
    on her hill-top above Lucena;
There being Virgins of the hill-tops and Virgins of the springs in
    Andalusia,
        while in Estremadura
The Virgins are dryads, and live in the oak-trees,
    of whom maybe later

Baraka, indeed, is an accumulated strength
    'from spending the long winter months
Of solitary and uneventful life
    in voluntary seclusion and self-absorption',
Appearing for its moment
    in the guise of sudden inspiration,
A phantom that all artists in all or any of the arts
    know well is non-existent

But, as well,
    baraka has, I believe another meaning
    of smiling good fortune and of giving pleasure;
Was this not, in parenthesis,
The name of the beautiful *sheikhat*,
    or Berber dancing-girl from Tiznit or Goulimine,
Moroccan towns of the Sud, famous for their dancers,
    whom we saw perform
In the palace of El Glaoui at Marrakesh,
    in long silken dress with wide sleeves, and white silk turban?
Her beauty and Liotard-like smoothness,
    as of scented petal,
Must long since have faded

Nostalgia can be among the worst of all neuroses:
  I had a brother and a sister,
And the *baraka* and its antithesis
  Were on our beginnings,
With potency both forwards and backwards in our lives,
And in our doubled selves as writers and as persons
  which there was no more avoiding
Than of escaping one's own shadow

And where of late,
  as to the first person singular?
Only four months ago in the Apulian spring
  and in the air and country of the *trulli*,
Where the clusters of conical-roofed, one-roomed,
Round, whitewashed beehive-huts
  populating the entire landscape,
Portended the storing and garnering of the cornstooks,
With half-a-lifetime of poems still unpublished,
  a literary testament untaken,
And I wondered whether, or not,
  my *baraka* were leaving me

Hoping for a little time more
  before the darkness,
Oblivious, not of beliefs, but of religions;
Drawn like the humming-bird to the hibiscus,
  another and another time;
Changing theme, it could be too often,
  trying at other flowers,
As though there were ever nectar anew upon the morning,
Which is the truth, but not the whole truth,
  any more than there is sugar in the ice-cap,
Or comfort in Arctic and Antarctic Poles of loneliness
  and inaccessibility,

But in fact the *baraka* of the Moors
  as a spiritual balm or ointment
Has been of general application,
Until it fails and turns sour,
  as with 'a noble Moor in the service of the Venetian State',
Or city of the lagoons,
Where, in the last generation
  before the *baraka* of the Venetians had deserted them,
The white-stallion'd quadrigas
Will be circling, touching down through sun-drenched clouds
  upon the painted ceilings

Let me think, by contrary,
    of how my *baraka* has befriended me,
Smoothing my way under the strawberry-nets
    and among the gallicas and damascenas,
For what little that was worth,
    being but the foretaste or sip of poetry,
Since the difficulty as with opera composers
    is in finding a libretto that gives opportunity,
Which,
    when that happens,
Must be taken with both hands
    and ten or a dozen poems written in as many days

As in the old opera, the work of a fortnight,
    when the *baraka* of the moonlight comes down
And the theatre darkens
    for Lindoro to prelude on the strings
At the beginning of his serenade;
As, too, in the plangent plucking of the violins
    for the start of the sextet in *Lucia*,
Which is as much of a *coup de théâtre*
As that moment when Lady Macbeth
    'enters, reading a letter',
To dead silence from the orchestra in Verdi's opera:—
A pair of instances of the *baraka* at work
    in the false moonlight of the stage

2

There is a *baraka* upon all fourteen
    of the mature piano concertos of Mozart,
No fewer than six of them written in one year,
    the year of the *Nozze di Figaro*,
And equivalent to a human civilization on their own,
    the rest of his works apart,
With animal high spirits, poignant sadnesses,
Ordered ecstacies,
    unheard of elegancies,
His world within his world in variation form,
The mimic hunt with flurry of horns
    and galloping hooves,
Or mock-military panache for the finale

From which cosmogony of marvels
    and the mystery of their creation,

And with the town of *Carmen*, of *Figaro* and *Don Giovanni* still
      in mind,
There could be a *baraka* on the orange-trees
      for their being in fruit and blossom everywhere at one and the
      same time;
And even, in diminuendo,
That there were,
      there probably still are,
Mechanical pianos in the wine-shops of Seville,
Several of them playing at once,
      grinding out the tawdry, but spangled tunes
But never now in London
      a *baraka* of the barrel-organs,
The churning, churning of their metal tongues,
      and the slow move off into the distance   •
Looking up at windows for coppers thrown down.
      Are there still, I wonder, in the town where I was born,
Booths for pierrots on the tidal sands,
Or the wet-weather, indoors Catlin's Arcadia
      that I remember?

Bach's Organ Preludes and Fugues

In another world of the senses,
      approaching *Bach's Organ Preludes and Fugues*
As sacred buildings, no less so
      than the cathedrals or Burgos or Toledo,
Not built haphazard, but of arithmetical design and purpose,
      and not exclusively of religious feeling:—
As that fugue which ends triumphantly, ecstatically,
      with the three notes I interpreted as Q.E.D.,
Quod Erat Demonstrandum
      as for the conclusion and proving of an Euclidean problem

Or another fugue,
      a pronouncement of the three names of God
From booming, wall-shaking and shuddering bell-tower
      and steeple of steeples
Over the shining and wet roofs of the North;
And a fugue that portrays, I would like to think, the Pentecostal
   Storm
      accompanying the Holy Spirit,
Controlled, but appalling in the thund'rous welkin

Or, yet another in innocent and happy laughter,
    as of the maidens of Saturn
Dancing barefoot,
    decorously clad of course, in crocus'd meadows;
Or a fugue more like a kitten playing with a ball of wool,
    and there is no more hope of the skein escaping her
Than that the mouse will get away
    while 'pensive Selima' is in playful mood
With armature of teeth and claws,
    but soft velvet paws

On a Seldom-Performed Entr'acte from Tchaikovsky's *The Sleeping Beauty*

Entr'acte, 'with prominent solo violin
    to cover the necessary change of scene',
Which is that of stage transition
    to a sleeping world
While the audience waits in semi-darkness,
    a sleeping world,
Supposedly lying sleeping for a hundred years,
    waiting to be woken:—
A score that we are told
    only took six weeks in all to compose and finish,
And this entr'acte added at the last moment,
    sketched out and orchestrated in a matter of hours,
Has an overpowering undertone of anguish and nostalgia

Opening,
    with 'lay-out' like the slow movement of a violin concerto
To conventional sawing and pleading of the instrument,
But already,
    it inspires him and catches fire,
The music grows poignant and impassioned,
And by the time the theme comes back again
    and takes over,
The soaring, soaring of the virtuoso has begun,
    and the composer's extraordinary gift for identifying
    himself
With the emotions of his characters is apparent

It is only sad and despairing
    that Tchaikovsky wasted so much of his life
Upon his symphonies,
    for the flowering of his lyrical genius,
His temperament and the high fever of his nostalgia
    are in *Eugène Onegin*, and in this music we are hearing,
Where he can involve himself
    without too exact a statement of his involvement,
Made the more thrilling for him
    because of the *barricades mystérieuses* of the footlights,
Over which he could project himself through his music
    unequivocally into their midst,
Induce his own feelings into the singers or the dancers,
    share their emotions with them,
And absorb them back again

Himself,
    disembodied for the moment,
And inhabiting first one, then other
    of his own embodiments or transformations;
As now,
    in the darkened theatre,
Transferring his own emotions mostly felt in ambiguity,
    but no less strong for that,
From the young 'prince' or *jeune premier* of the fairy story
    to the 'princess' or ballerina,
At this moment lying in darkness and discomfort
    on a makeshift bed-of-state behind the curtains,
Whom he must awaken with a kiss and bring to life
    at the climax of the music,
Which becomes inspired by the transfer of affections
    and the throbbing excitement and anticipation leading to it
Much as the playwright,
    we may be thinking,
Veers first to Antony, then Cleopatra
    among the splendours of his imagination
In 'the affairs of Egypt'

'Little Dark Magician of the Clavichord'

(To Violet Gordon Woodhouse)

Of which wonderland of music
    I tried to write the best I could,
With always at back of my mind
    'the little dark magician of the clavichord',
A dear friend I loved, and heard play for thirty years,
    who was no musical pedant and not a scholiast,
But with a memory
    amounting to total recall of music she had ever known,
A player beyond equal in Bach and in Mozart,
    and in sonatas by Domenico Scarlatti

But besides all this,
    more than all else perhaps,
In her unimaginable rendering of little pieces
Of which the effect would be totally lost
    if played upon a piano;
Such as, old songs
    like 'Dover Camp', or 'Tell me, Daphne', of Giles
  Farnaby;
'Chesapeake and Shannon', a sailor's song;
    'The Willow Song' from Verdi's *Othello*;
Or 'Scots wha hae', this last
    more spirited than were believable;
In all of which
    she must have resembled, I think,
In effect, however different in idiom,
    that forgotten virtuoso of the cymbalom,
And been thereby twice over,
    among the greatest of solo players there has ever been

I believe the secret in her performance
    of these little encore pieces in such perfection
Being the impeccable gradations
    of tone and timing only attainable, it may be,
On the clavichord, which she called
    'the most beautiful solo instrument ever invented,
And the study of a lifetime'

The Magical History of Mother Goose

'All men and women come home at evening'
   and the two old friends and lovers
Read the words above the porch
   of the church I would not, could not ever find again
But said nothing, did not speak,
Their days quickening, hurrying to the end:—
She, an old woman
Who had played to me that morning
Music of such immortal youth and freshness
I wanted to cry out loud

When we got back to the tall old house
   in the July evening and the fire was lit,
We had supper and more music
And at last as the fire flickered that same piece again
   by the musician who died at thirty-five,
Half-way from youth to age

This little adagio from a piano sonata
   is a quintessence of his genius
In his early twenties, in the elixir of his youth,
   who knew the opera house
And was in love at the time
   with a sixteen-year old opera singer
In the false sunlight of the theatre

And that evening, or the next,
   when the fire was lit
We looked at the little boys skating
   in top hats
In the old chap book
And drew the curtains
And took down *The Magical History of Mother Goose*

Oh! the beauty of her thatched cottage
Under the trees
With tall hollyhocks and honeysuckle
At her door
And we see the crone in her steeple hat

Sitting in the kitchen
Her black cat beside her

A stranger from London
Comes to her door:
Her cloak and stick
And witch's hat hanging on the wall

The kettle is boiling
The tall clock is ticking
And the old chap-book
Turns into a pantomime
The beautiful glittering daughter
Sitting beside me
Turned the page
And the magical story
Knew neither youth nor age

Oh! the beauty of the tall house
And the magic in it
In the panelled room
The fire flickered
There was magic in the room

The immortal youth and freshness
Of the music
Played in my ears
As I lay thinking
All night long

Music I heard again
At Las Huelgas
Among the white-robed nuns
At practise in the choir
With a nun at a small organ
Among the tomb chests
Of Infantas and Plantagenet Princesses

Oh! how I remembered then,
The little dark musician
And woman of genius long dead
And the evening of music
In the tall old house
With the glittering beauty of twenty
At my side

Music of deceptive innocence
For it is only the music
That stays young

While we mortals
Will meet, having met,
Or will not meet again

Sandalwood Song

Sweet clavichord
Of whom the keys are ribs
And your body its casket
Made of sandalwood

Magical instrument now with open lid
Waiting, lying still,
For fingers to touch the notes . . .

The Sousedská is Playing Through the Summer Trees

The sousedská
Is playing through the summer trees
On this sunflower evening
Dance
    that is entraining and entrancing

Danced by couples
A dance of turning, turning
Not a ländler or slow waltz
    nor a mazurka
But the opening bars of a waltz
    with the long beats of a mazurka

Danced
    with slow gliding step
A bow or obeisance at the end of every phrase
Stately and formal
    as the polonaise

Sousedská
    there is whispering and sighing
Sighing and whispering in the name
And it as if the tune came towards you
    arms full of flowers
Then, a turn in the music
And it is as though you are looking
    in a lovely face

The graceful, slow turn
    of the sousedská
And now the tune comes back
A little accented
    in the brass

Sousedská in flower
    in the summer evening
Sousedská
    that plays itself into your arms
And lies there
As if you are looking
    in a lovely face

'If music be the food of love, play on'

If music be the food of love, play on;
Give me excess of it, that, surfeiting,
The appetite may sicken and so die.
That strain again! it had a dying fall:
O, it came o'er my ear like the sweet sound
That breathes upon a bank of violets,
Stealing and giving odour! Enough, no more,
'Tis not so sweet now as it was before.

                        Twelfth Night

'That strain again! it had a dying fall',
    one of the magical tricks of music
Denied the poet
    who can but write on,
Hoping if ever to cause a catch of breath
    as in the opening words of the play,
Wherein we confuse the poet with the lutenist
    and can believe we are listening to his song.

'Give me excess of it, that, surfeiting,
The appetite may sicken and so die'
    vain hope for once taken
One never tires, and only calls for more;
Music it is true being then in infancy,
    as in its 'teens,
'Like the sweet sound upon a bank of violets
    stealing and giving odour'

In his opening words to *Twelfth Night*
    the poet shows impatience and mistrust of music
Calling even for excess of it
    so that 'the appetite may sicken and so die'.
Then relating as to the breath of wild flowers,
    even confusing this with the beauty of it, scent with sound,
'Stealing and giving odour';
And once more condemning music as it steals upon the ear
    'Enough, no more.
    'Tis not so sweet now as it was before'

It is as if he had a grudge against music,
    more than he ever showed against his actors,
As though jealous of its potentialities
    that music could clog and delay the playwright's action:—
Having had his fill of it,
First singing till his voice broke,
    could it be?
Then, put to a stringed instrument in the minstrel's gallery?
And all considered what was music in his time
    compared to the world he had now embarked upon?

Were we to listen to the singer in his song,
    it would be of country flowers
That were not inimical to towns;

Of soft-cheek indument of primrose,
　　of cowslip breath,
Pink-franked integument of carnation
　　and the commonplaces of the rose

Not here,
　　the 'tulip cheeks' in highest compliment
To Abbasid maidens their contemporaries
　　if eternally indolent and idle,
By the fountains and cypresses of Shiraz
　　or at the turquoise vaults of Isfahan

2

The greatest of poets
　　came with the first plays to be written,
And transcended the music of his age,
Music being but the condiment to poetry,
　　as we can read in his treatment of it,
Though he may have had innate understanding
　　of what it could attain to in another time

Once the music of the Italians had turned to opera,
　　music of the theatre, that is to say,
And no longer sacred music or the featured masque,
　　they could work their magic:—
The Italian tenor in the person of such singers
　　as Mario or Rubini
Being the most finished instrument ever perfected
For conveying intimation of human physical love
　　from male actor to the females in the audience;
And were there but trained naturalists
　　in another race of beings,
We would value their learned account of the phenomenon
　　as in a nature film of courting and display habits among the
　　birds

A perfect understanding of Italian is not necessary
　　in order to get the message of the tenor's serenade,
A convention which may have become almost a joke by this
　　time,
　　and could be one of the reasons why Verdi
Who had a native distrust of tenors
　　always of instinct gave his heroic roles to baritones

'Show Boat'

Remembering now,
    where it is a question of inspiration, so called, or of
possession.
The anthropomorphic figures of early men
Hunting in deerskins in the cave-paintings of Les Eyzies,
    a ritual which is the beginning of the theatre
And of all acting;
The magical dressing up and 'donning of the robe',
    the rôle too of the officiating priest in all religions,
As, here, of the musician who inhabits
    and is in entire possession of the music,
Of ourselves, the audience, the virtuoso and the actor

And not otherwise really
    than as the waggon of the Thespians,
A farm cart
    on which was erected a temporary stage,
Arriving from the vineyard
    with the first actors,
All a little drunken,
    their faces daubed and dyed
With lees of wine

Or the pierrots of childhood
    in their trestle-theatre on the sands,
Their every performance,
    as though they had never been,
Washed away, obliterated by the incoming tide

There being a first
    and a last for everything,
As we will know ourselves
    one night or day;
And now
    to the sush-szush of paddle-wheels
Here comes the floating theatre
    that plays the river towns,
Approaching through the sunset
    in a blaze of lights,

Music pouring from her decks and portholes,
    down the lazily flowing,
The Southern drawl of waters
To music of unaccustomed sort,
    or so it seemed then,
Even if only an imitation,
    or improvement on the old music,

And an entertainment of 'make belief'
    playing in several senses at once,
As we will see

For the tunes themselves,
    the imitation tunes,
Are already fifty years old,
    they date from 1925,
Written it was the intention
    in the popular idiom of fifty years before

Just how old,
    would someone have to be,
Now,
    who was in his twenties in 1925,
And remembers the tunes and words?

So it could be this evening,
    or fifty,
Or a hundred years ago,
And it is 'make believe'
    and again make 'believe'
All night till morning

There being the two schools aboard,
    the Sacred and Profane,
And it veers from one school to the other:—
    but which is the more serious?
For one can 'make belief'
    and soon find you are not pretending,
Or lose your 'belief' in most things
    and discover you are not less happy

Meantime,
    aboard the Show Boat,
Call it the 'Ship of Fools',

A deck that I have trod before,
    attended a banquet on board ship,
And slept in cabins
    down in the bowels of the vessel
To never ceasing music
    as in the Paris night clubs,
'jusqu'à l'aube,' 'till dawn',
It is one huge stage
    with someone for ever singing of love,
Sometimes in chorus
    as if they almost believe what they are singing

With the nostalgic theme-song playing in our ears,
    for there were tunes then
Which carried one along with them,
    and have the power of bringing back the image of their
    time:—
'Smoke gets in your eyes' being another of the tunes

In the last breath of a summer night
    did the words of the song take on a meaning?
And all was not pretence?
How is one to tell,
    when all is but 'make belief' and acting?

Call it once more the 'Ship of Fools'
    'the barge that burn'd on the water
In the love-sick winds',
Where one of love's torments
    is the see-saw of love,
Apostrophized in the words of the song
    they are singing

'Let's make believe you love me,
Let's make believe
            that I love you':—
    changing to
'Let's make believe I love you
Let's make believe
            that you love me

And the music repeats again and again,
    as if it is only the present that counts
And there is no future
Aboard the 'Ship of Fools'
    where all is but 'make belief' and acting

Preferring,
    none the less,
To stay aboard
Listening to the music
    which at least is tuneful,
And wandering on the wings of it
    which way it takes us

So let it be
    that we are only moving,
Nightly,
    to another and different audience
A little further up or down the river

As again,
    to the sush-szush-sush of paddle wheels,
Here comes the floating theatre
    that plays the river towns,
Approaching through the sunset
    and in a blaze of lights,
Music pouring from her decks and portholes,
Down the lazily flowing,
    the Southern drawl of waters,
And the Show Boat of Mississippi
    puts in to shore

Harlequinade

Two Themes, Taken one at a Time

1

Remembering this morning
    the retired chemist living in South London
Who painted clowns' faces
    upon 'blown' eggshells
In order to record their 'make up':—
    and I think had a hand in designing them, as well;
The eggs were on show
    at an exhibition of *Clowns and Clowning*:—
And I thought them as beautiful in idea
As the most perfect and exquisite
    of eighteenth-century snuff-boxes
Fetching tens of thousands of pounds,
    if of less intrinsic worth
Than 'the hundred-year-old eggs' of Chinese gourmets.

This,
    on a day when I am without an idea of my own of any
    kind:—
And I take up an old notebook
    to find,
'G. Voorhelm, Haarlem, 1773, gives a list
    of 246 named varieties of double hyacinths,
Of which fewer than half-a-dozen
    are now in cultivation'.

2

And to take the two themes,
    one by one:—
Spangled gowns and breeches (galligaskins)
    were on view,
Worn by clowns with the starched ruff
    of Sir Walter Raleigh,
Or the Conde de Orgaz of the Toledan painting;
There were sack-like trousers
    for the comic clowns to run in,

And big boots lent by Coco Junior
    made on a special last
Costing (then!) about eighteen pounds
    from a firm
Whose address 'was a closely guarded family secret'

Midget Clown's Dress, Tramp Umbrella,
    Comedy Bowler which squirts water,
Smoky, Tony Tina and Boby,
    all clowns' names:—
But the clowns,
    even the Augustes
Who 'try to help' with the matting
    and get rolled up in it,
Are always more than a little frightening and alarming:—
Even the lovable and droll Grock
    was not to be trifled with
By his violinist partner and precursor,
    who came on first, so impeccably dressed,
But in vexation
    struck that bald pate with his violin bow,
And must take the consequences

And ever and always the pierrot-clowns
    with floured faces and the features of poets,
That, knowing poets as I know them,
    there have never been:—
Not in this world,
    or if ever,
Only in the world of the theatre and of music:—

And yet come nearer to the immortal Pierrot
    down the long gallery of the Louvre;
Look up into his face
    and you will see Le Grand Gilles
Has red eyelids and has been weeping,
    maybe for no good reason,
    but all the reason more:—
And it is not by mistake
    the painter has put red in the corners of his eyes

To the Self-Portrait of A. Watteau Playing the Hurdy-Gurdy

For whom did you paint your own portrait
    as a man playing a hurdy-gurdy,
Haunter of the coulisses and lover of the *Comédie Vénitienne*,
    your portrait on a panel not much bigger than a postcard,
Master of the *sanguine*,
    and most finished draughtsman there has ever been?

In the painting you are a young man
    in your 'thirties. Pinched and thin:
Already dying. As you grind the handle
    of the hurdy-gurdy
We hear you coughing.

A hurdy-gurdy is a wretched instrument
    and only a droning, wheezing imitation
Of music: little more than a box on a stick.
But was it better than nothing?
What was the secret? Is it in the tune?

In the word 'hurdy-gurdy', reader, do you not hear it,
    grinding, turning?
Now. There. There. Just then?
    with limping, halting walk.
Nearer, nearer. And gone now,
    or moved down the street?

Hurdy-gurdy is *'una ghironda'* in Italian,
    lover of the coulisses and haunter of the *Comédie Italienne*,
In the old opera which has songs with hurdy-gurdy
    accompaniment
        it runs; *'che ascolto? . . . e questa musica?*
'Io la conosco: il suono della ghironda.'

Let it play on for a moment,
    till we hear the hurdy-gurdy in the street outside;
'Il suono della ghironda di Pierotto',
    and a voice begging.

'*Soccorrete povero Savoiardo*
Poveretto abbandonato', his beggar's cry;
Then his song,
    ending '*Addio, Addio*',
And the hurdy-gurdy whines down and dies.

Or do I hear it start again,
    and Pierotto begging?

The hurdy-gurdy and the beggar's cry
    haunt the little painting:
And the painting haunts the haunted hurdy-gurdy
    and Pierotto's song:
I cannot part them in my mind.
            (The opera is Donizetti's *Linda di Chamounix*)

Pedrolino

Pedrolino!
    Poor Pedrolino!
Some sort of Pierrot
    from *Le Théâtre Italien* of Riccoboni;
It is no difficult part to play
    just to stand there with uplifted hands
In despairing sorrow and dismay.

What is the import of it all?
    Pedrolino!
That I may have felt like you
    all that lifetime ago?

In the wood
    (where I never set foot!)
That was rose-pink with primroses
    which are naturalized nowhere else in the world
But in this one wood along the smooth-flowing river,
    where deep runs the river and dark lies the shade;
Where I heard the woodpecker
    deep in the wood (and in imagination)
A ghostly knocking
    which was the knocking in the prompter's box

Pedrolino!
>Who will never live to be as old as I am.
To know as much,
>or understand as little,
But had the harlequins
>in their five attitudes around him

Pedrolino!
>Poor Pedrolino!
Who now becomes Pierotto
>in Donizetti's *Linda di Chamounix,*
And we hear
>*'Il suono della ghironda',*
The grinding of his hurdy-gurdy
>as he moves away

Farewell Song

(from Les Trois Cousins, *1702)*

The 'drop'
>is to allow a few moments between acts,
And the whole company crosses from left to right
>across the stage,
While the drama moves into the haystooks
Seen from my bedroom window
>and it thunders,
August-thunder a village or two away.

It is inconsequent as all dreams
But the encampment or empty fairground fills
>for the dancers of Sfessania;
We see,
Her who was nearer to Callot than any living figure in the theatre,
With parrot-mask
>taking her curtain,
Fingering the limp feathers in her hat
>to a few steps of the Charleston.*

* Nellie Wallace

84

But was that thunder?
Thunder does not throb and sigh like that.
    Or do we hear the lion-skin drums of the Ciganje?
The tinkers 'Snap' and 'Pedro'
Dance to the tune of Calino Casturame,
    an 'Irish air'
That our archers sang on the eve of Agincourt
Where are the skewbald genets of the tinkers
    Tethered below the castle walls?

And now it is Mlle Desmares
    whom Watteau loved
Known for her pretty voice and delightful way of laughing
    who comes to the footlights with the full company round her
To sing her song:
    'Venez dans l'île de Cythère
    En pèlerinage avec nous,
    Jeune fille n'en revient guère
    Ou sans amant ou sans époux;
    Et on y fait sa grande affaire
    Des amusements les plus doux.'
It is Mlle Desmares but we do not clearly see her face.

It brings the yew trees
    and the white damson of Calino Casturame into my eyes and
ears
Even the ghost of the syringa cannot hold me
    I go on board at once
Across the gangplank into the galleon
    but, in fact,
Landing on it from a rowing-boat
And beset immediately by touts and guides.

Another Isola Bella
    in more azure waters
Climbing in ten terraces a hundred feet above the lake
With the cork trees, lemons, oranges,
    camellias, oleanders,
The white peacocks,
Shell-grottoes, arbours, statues
    of Mercutio's dew-dropping south
Where time is infinite.
And on which stage or terrace will they perform?
I look for the Escalera Dorada,
    or 'golden staircase' down to the Cathedral floor of Burgos.

All of Armida's galleon is a theatre,
    and not a theatre,
The frogs are croaking in the grottoes,
The fireflies are coming in sortie out of the myrtle-thickets,
    circling,
Showing their lights, not making landings
Were we deep in the wood we would hear the young nightingales
    at practice.
It gets dark and one hears the fountains
As in the Italy I loved and knew
It seizes me again and takes me
Though I was not happy on the shores of Maggiore all those years
    ago.
        and now all Italy is stained and smeared with Mussolini.

Oh! for the Italy of the Popes and Doges
Of the Medici Grand Dukes and the Bourbon Kings!
I hear the wheezing of a hurdy-gurdy
    in the scented nightfall,
But whoever was playing it
Turns his back and walks away.

For a Floral Inebriation

'O rose with two hearts'

O rose with two hearts
What would you say to me
Rose with the double heart
That grows on the white rose-tree?

Rose that blossomed
And was Heaven-sent;
Where are the syllables
For your petals and your scent?

Rose held in my hand
Now, more far off than the moon
Long after my meridian
Though early in my afternoon

I will find you
And your turn will come;
There are all the sorts of roses
And we will hear them, one by one

The rose-voice
Out of each rose-tower
Will be the rose-scent
Of every rose-bower
And so at last
White rose on fire

I'll hold you once more
Before I tire

And know your secret
And ask you for the answer

White rose!
For those few summers only;
Divine acrobat
And dancer!

Rosa gallica (Monsieur Pellisson)

Tree of pink roses
What wrist of dew
Came round in the night
And quartered you?

Sliced you like an orange
Or a pomegranate?

Each rose a half-globe,
Or half an astrolabe;
Half an armillary sphere
Or half the atmosphere;

Sliced with a star-ray for a knife
And a moonbeam for a kitchen table;

As half the moon,
Or the New World across the ocean;
Each rose his opportunity
His ambition and his notion

That dewy wrist
One imagines or supposes
Tried to navigate
Among the roses

Held to his course
And would not let go
In the sweet-breathing
Archipelago

So many paired wonders
On the one rose-tree
Not an iota between them
In scent or symmetry

Who can he be, this rosomane,
Who prefers his roses cut in twain;

His wrist of dew
Our only clue;
And that of one rose
He makes two?

Rosa centifolia (?)

Rose of a hundred petals
That are as battlements
And machicolations,
Where only a beetle walks as sentinel,
Rose-parapets and crenellations;
Rose
Of keep and donjon as a Crusader's castle

With rosebuds for curtain towers,
And sharp thorns for fortifications,
Is there a Princess to rescue
And ransom from the Saracens?

Or rose-myrrh
And cassia and frankincense,
Rose-sandalwood
(And it makes more sense
Rubbed with your own oil-of-roses);
Are your petals
The wrapped bandages to hide your heart;
Rosy-integument and carapace,
Embalmed in its own mummy-case?

Just why,
This heavenly smell;
Soft rose-face,
Nest,
And cradle for the nightingale?

'Hebe's Lip': (Rosa damascena rubrotincta)

Red-lipp'd handmaiden
Smelling of a wild rose;
Restorer of youth and strength
To gods and men;
Rose of the golden anthers!

O red-lipp'd rose that sits upon a knee
And lets fall her petals wantonly,
Not many petals, being lightly clad,
Fauness
And apple-cheek'd Hamadryad!

Remember Iolas,
I say, remember him,
My nympholept and paradigm;
Remember Iolas,
And what you did for him!

Harness your mother's chariot,
'Whenever requisite',
Put wine on board and fecund lettuces:
Whip up her peacocks,
We'll ride with Juno to the dewponds and the haycocks;

And at the picnic
Pour nectar for me,
While pouring nectar
You need but slip and fall.

One knew of old
That there were limbs to roses;
But your *tutu* of two rows of petals
Tilts;
And what it then discloses

Makes the god dismiss you from his service
And put Ganymede to pour his liquor,
As though your rose-waist is a disservice
And your rose-hips an imposture;

But red-lipp'd Hebe,
They are nothing of the kind;
We but ask of you to shed your petals;
It is the shedding of the rose
That inspires, and in the same breath unsettles.

'Rose with no name'

Who ever heard of a brass band
With doubled instruments,
And the players are rose-attars
And rose-chromosomes?
This is the rose which grows with me,
But has no name.
Of profound
And flaring crimson,
So enjoying itself
That sometimes it bursts its calyx,
Or even the green eye of the rose
Is not in the middle;
But when the firing of this rose-rocket
Is successful,
The sky rains with rose-parachutes
Descending.

Rose-umbrellas
Turned inside out
Caught
Face upwards on the briars;
Roses
Of loaded crimson full up to the brim;
Huge vol-aux-vents
Of roses,
Double helpings that taste not,
But instead have scent
To touch upon the senses,
So that in its day
One thinks of little but the rose
That has no name.

Rosa muscosa: Baron de Wassenaer

To breathe into a face
What is that? What else could it be
But a rose?
Yes! a rose. Yet listen:
There is nothing now but the immediacy
Of breathing in your face and person
Ah! now, and now again.
And now too late!
I am hopeless now
And do not care what happens:
Yet once more, and once again,
In mimic of the action,
And to pretend – in vain
I loved the scent more than the person.

Rosa eglanteria rubiginosa: 'Janet's Pride'

During the mornings
    and evenings of the eglantine,
There are single, white blossoms,
And now and again a pink rose briar
Along the hedges and down the Green Lanes;
But it is the pink wild roses
That lift the heart as though it were a bird singing,
Wild pink roses with the yellow stamens.
While the dark bird sings its love calls
    and its amens

Rose briar taller than myself,
With all the airs aromatic for a few feet round you,
Not from your rose smell, but from the smell of the leaves,
Being no lover of single flowers,
I had hardly looked at you!

Rose briar taller than I am,
And sweetbriar from the hedges,
There is this difference,
Your flowers are white in the centre
And have rosy edges

Where, and how did this happen?
Who found you,
        past a magpie cottage
In a Cheshire lane;
Had the Gypsies lit their fires,
And left their old boots behind,
When he,
        or she came back again?

Rose-tree
        of roses like as many solar systems,
Each with a cluster of suns
        or parhelions for a centre;
Rose-tree
        like perpetual dawn all day long,
And called after a maiden in the imagination

Rose of the morning
        and the evening,
Each petal of the miraculous rose-edging;
Wild rose of dawn,
Awake before the hedgers have begun their hedging

Rosa officinalis: The Red Rose of Lancaster: Rosa gallica maxima

Rose
        perhaps the oldest of our rose-lines,
In all the glory of your yellow stamens
        and flowers of clear crimson without mark or stain

By now twice illegitimate,
        for what that matters,
Red rose
        and parent to Fair Rosamund

93

Red rose of the portcullis,
     from whom I have a drop of that rose-blood in my veins,
Or am at least brother to that pretendant,
     Now fading, falling as we all must

I have not yet felt the drag or weight,
     but for how much longer can that be,
Who have still your pollen
     though I cannot pollinate?

Blackspot and rust are all around to see
     the wrecks of two persons are all that now remains,
Whom I loved more than they loved me

But the beauty and poetry
     I learned from her
Are antidote to all self-pity

Rosa francofurtana

Soft centenarian,
Now known to be four times as old as that,
     and not ageing, never altering,
I would not wish your secret,
     or not the whole of it,
But only to go back a little way, a step or two,
I would not have your secret,
And be left alone in time

Would it not be better,
     most beautiful of roses,
To keep with your own kind,
Better to die younger,
     and be long dead by now?
But a rose answered,
     the rose that died early,
And scarcely could remember me,

Or so I thought,
     till in the scent of the rose
I heard my name.
     and the rose:

'I remember you.
You did not choose. I chose;
and how could I know
What was to become of me?'

Rosa polyantha (?)

Rose,
    brought here from Renishaw,
Some old sort of *polyantha* covered with flowers
    and smelling of cream,
When I look at you
I see Augusts of thirty, forty, even fifty years ago;
I hear
    the shunting of coal-trucks behind the lake
And can smell the pits;
Where we look down into the wilderness,
    past warrior and Amazon, along privet and holly
The cornfields of Clowne are white on the skyline,
    and slowly, slowly,
Then with a rush the past comes back again

Rosebeds
    of the lower garden,
In a golden evening after tea;
Rosebeds
    between the yew pyramids
And near the clematis;
Roses
    I do not care for,
But they bring back the ghosts:—
Music which made the keep of Bolsover
    to be in Poland near the coal-mines
In the month of wild raspberries;
And a darkness comes up from Sheffield
    like the end of things

Rose of the Entr'acte

Rose of an entr'acte
    from Strauss's *A Thousand and One Nights*,
And we breathe in a deep, deep breath of it
    which lasts
Until the passionate climax and tension of the music,
    and dies down
Till it is lifeless and lies still;
Long-drawn sadness and melancholy of the Waltz King,
    which takes breath into itself and begins again
While we are still face to face with the rose

Music of the lit theatre and summer bandstand,
    with the violin of the Gypsy primás,
If we listen for it,
    always in the air and never far away;
Which if it would only quicken and catch fire
    in the csárdás of the Hungarians
Could tell us everything

But we hear the entr'acte bell,
    if only in our imagining;
And comes the electric moment,
When, holding his bow in his right hand
    he gives the beat,
Moment which was among the sensations of all music,
    a sacred or suspended silence,
The shape and limits of which have given up their souls to
    him,
    and in the next instant,
Is leading the orchestra with his violin

So take, too, the rose
    and hold it in your fingers,
It yields up its soul to you
    that is all in itself and has no more to say;
Rose of the entr'acte and all history,
That though in the bed of Cleopatra
    Keeps its secret and its mystery,

And can hardly with any delight
    raise up a ghost for you,
The ghost of a rose

Rose of Two Hearts

Rose of two hearts
One soon forgets you in the semi-tropics;
All is fiercer,
There is no forgiveness:
As it is with flowers
So it is with men and women
The dead must be buried by next evening

So it is with the yellow hibiscus
That is born in the morning and dead by nightfall,
And the yellow with fire on its petals
Of first dawn,
And the double rose
That is two roses in one

I have read of the Rumanian Ciganje
That they like their drums made of lion-skin
Because that is said to throb and sigh
When beaten;
So it is with the heat here at mid-day
Between the lion-skies of morning and evening

The Ciganje carry the big drums
To attract spectators to their street performances
Their children turn cartwheels
And are trained tumblers

Here it begins early
The yellow acrobats are already
Turning, spinning
Dawn has all the hues of the hibiscus
Till it becomes the lion-skin morning

The yellow
The stained yellow the double rose

Are bending back in the heat
Are curving reflexing their petal limbs
In pleasure

In the beating, throbbing
Of mid-day
The yellow the double rose are holding their attitudes
Are bending their petals quite inside out
In ecstasy

Disk of five pistils
And protruding stamen of the hibiscus
Are not only for enjoyment
But for some other purpose
Interrogation of the heat?
Who knows?
They do not know themselves
For they are dead by evening

Here are flowers that live and die
In a day
The yellow hibiscus and the tawny one
Are wilting

Rose of two worlds
That is two roses in one
Rose of the meridian
This is no theatre for your northern colouring
While the lion-skin drums are beating

I have not forgotten you
O rose of two worlds,
When the double rose,
That is two roses in one,
Is sleeping

Negros Superbe

Negros Superbe
Noir Véritable, Nigritienne
Hyacinth of Niger

In as many tints of porphyry,
Noir Véritable
Ebony of the hyacinths
A Negro in a foreign town
None know him
All are staring at his dark face and gown
Nigritienne Negress of the market-place
Talking and chattering in a flowered dress
Fair Negress dark dark
Fair none-the-less
Smooth body like the long stem of a lily
Small head Nigritienne thin wrists
Neat curls and plaitings of your Negress hair
O dark dark hyacinth dark as jet
O lovely blackbird lying in a net
Negros Superbe
Othello of the blue lilies
Blue Sultan of the tincturing herb
Four shillings and he is yours
The Sultan of the hyacinths and his turban.

L'Honneur d'Amsterdam

Huge lily of the landlocked waters
Pride of Amsterdam's red daughters
Born in the Venice of red bricks
Fair-bosom'd
Venus genetrix
Huge lily of Holland
Where there is no wood or hill
Himalaya of the windowsill
Red dolomite
And hyacinth
Dyed fircomb of the terebinth
Indian ascetic
Of the bed of ashes
Brahmin of the window-sashes
Lily of the lacquered Indies
Hyacinth and pyramid and tower of honey
Dutchmen sell you for a piece of money

Lilium tigrinum splendens

Cyclic change
    and metamorphosis
Of a crimson and white lily
    into an entire pack of hounds,
All with protruding tongues
    dripping saliva

The white petals tabbied with a multitude
    of vermilion specks or spots
Which thicken into solid tigerings or papillae,
    or even fleshy nipples of red
Toward the green throat or gullet of the lily

And peering into that dog-mouth,
    nearly putting your head into the ten-inch lily,
What do you see?
Six pollen-bearing anthers
    wantonly dangling and swaying

With like number of vermilion stripes or bars
    upon the petals,
The digit 6 being in the logic of the lily family,
    in the sense that we human beings
Have two ears, ten finger-nails and so on,
    and in fact and indeed,
There are male and female in the anatomy of the lily

Lilium auratum

*(On a Nōh actor's costume of the Momayama period (1573–1615) embroidered with lilies
and Court carriages)*

On the brown kimono
    of an actor in a Nōh play
There are Court carriages embroidered,
    and huge boughs of lilies;

A masked actor,
 but what an entrance he must have made
With that stilted step of the Nōh actor;
 his dress,
All lilies and Court carriages!

The chief of the Mandan Red Indians of the plains
 rattled as he walked,
From his crest or headdress of war-eagles' quills
 that fell from the back of his forehead quite down to his
 feet;
But this actor coming towards us from the left-hand side
Masked masked
 slow slow
  with curious, stilted step
—was it the tread of a live or a dead person I heard
 on the last night I will ever spend at my old home?—
Past the painted pine tree that is the only scenery,
 onto the little stage,
Rustles and shakes with lilies

One huge lily-tree,
 all up his dress as high as his left shoulder;
Lily leaves flashing their backs and fronts;
Giant lilies nodding their flowers,
 as big or bigger than the wheels of the ox-carts,
Up and down the brown silk of his kimono

The lily is the Auratum,
 Golden-rayed Hill Lily of Japan,
With bowl-shaped flowers of waxy-white
 Do you not smell the lilies?
Golden-rayed and crimson-spotted,
 with protruding anthers;
Lilies all over his dress in and among the carriages

I can count six of the ox-carts on the back of his robe,
 they are two-wheeled ox-carts,
So that a ladder is needed to climb aboard;
 tethered ox-carts but without their oxen,
With black wheels and shafts – as if lacquered—
 but like a high Gypsy 'tilt-waggon';
The cabin of the ox-cart always painted green

And what do we see?
> There are long sleeves trailing,
Trailing on the ground
> out of the corners of the Court carriages;
So there are ladies and princesses
> invisible inside the ox-carts

The ladies like to trail their sleeves,
> it is the fashion,
Wearing as many as a dozen silk robes,
> of different dyes;
Each sleeve the longer as it lies closer to the wrist,
And one sleeve-arm made longer than the other
> according to which side of the carriage she is to sit

The lilies on his lilied robe
> are the masculine element it is evident;
And the ox-carts with their hidden inhabitants
> are drawn up waiting,
Ready for the bullocks to be put back in the shafts,
> when it is done,
And be walked, not driven lumbering away

It is a general, or mass mock-insemination
> from the lilies;
A shaking and a shedding-down of the lily-pollen;
A rattling of lilies at the inner chamber,
> or nectary,
From which the long sleeves are trailing

There are ox-carts all over his robe,
> up and down among the enormous flower-heads;
But now I see nothing but lily-anthers and huge stamens;
> dangling boughs
And stems of lilies,
Sleeves trailing out from the nectary
> in every Court carriage,
And I am dazed and drunk with lilies

Tulipa: La Mignonne de Dryshout

Upon a day
In Confucian Holland of the long tobacco pipes
Dutchmen's breeches Calvinists and Mennonites
It is clear dove-soft and very still
And a girl with blue eyes comes to the window
Listen! there is nothing else to hear
But a hammering in the shipyards
And Dutchmen's voices here and there
Tacitus tells of the Frisians
And their gold-yellow hair
The milkmaid stands at the door
In East-Indian chintzes
And a hat of glittering straw
A few weeks ago
How gay it was with painted sledges
Snow lay thick upon the window ledges
Holland lay still like a glass ship in a bottle
All the winter
The hyacinth bulb slept in the cupboard
Swan sledges chintz headdresses long print gowns
Faces fresh like roses in the little towns
The girl with blue eyes and fair flaxen hair
Tended the pale blue hyacinth
With the breath of honey
Till one morning
When the sun was yellow as new money
The girl and the hyacinth
Like two plants of blue lilies
Like a pair of pale hyacinths
Were the same
Mignonne de Dryshout was her name

Spellbinder

And as if from islands further west,
    deeper into the mists,
Not sea-green daffodils,
    but a green-yellow I had not known before,
Except in primroses,
    and then only in shadow near to the yews;
A green-yellow like starlight all morning through
    in the golden grove,
Paling the aureolin

But I have noticed that in a day or two
    the petals of this daffodil become white-pointed,
That their flanges where they join the tube
    and was never sign of needle or thread,
Are white-stained,
    that the trumpet has its bell-mouth whitened too,
As if from sleeping in starlight
    that gives pallor and engenders dreams

So,
    folded in its own greenness,
This cluster,
    this isle of daffodils,
Dreams,
    and soon dies away

Fritillary

Pay a shilling
To look at the fritillaries,
Thousands and thousands of them
All in this one field
Lanthorns of snakeskin,
Dangling, swaying,

Oh! the snakiness, the delicacy,
Of another,
   and another fritillary,
Hanging from its gallows-tree!

In term-time at Oxford
The Gypsies sold them
At the street-corner,
Near the evening papers,
Under the strip-lighting.
'Anyone living in the North or West
   outside the fritillary counties,
Should walk at least once in a fritillary field
   before he dies.'
Agreed! Agreed!

Why,
   why are fritillaries
'Very appropriate to Gypsies'?
Because their dark wrists
Set the lanterns shaking;
Lanterns, not to shed light,
But to let the sunlight through
All of snakeskin,
Of one green night's making.

Snaky locks? Oh! no! no!
Lanterns of snakeskin
And of plumskin;
   maybe,
Chamois-leather of myrobolan,
   or
Kidskin of bullace
And greengage, beaten thin,
Like sharkskin or shagreen;
Dappled, chamfered,
Dangling, swaying,
   fritillaries,
No sooner come, than gone,
   like
The dark 'travellers' along the rose-hung hedges.

Foxglove

(to the ghost of Violet Gordon Woodhouse playing Mendelssohn's Midsummer Night's Dream)

Foxglove,
Which means 'fairy' glove,
For whom to try on
Upon her hands,
One finger at a time?
And holding nettlestalks
For mallets,
Play upon the fairy cymbalom,
Or dulcimer,
Under a dockleaf tree?

Music
For Midsummer Night,
As dew falls
With the sound of distant horns,
O what is there in a spotted foxglove
That brings magic,
And makes us listen?
Look not around!
The hand of the little dark musician
Sweeps glissando
On the clavichord.

Jasmine of Hammamet

Jasmine,
　　white jasmine growing on the wall,
With the poignant sweet smell from it
　　reminding me of the jasmine of Hammamet
That we never saw growing,
　　nor indeed knew where it grew,

But every evening
    at about the hour we went up onto the roof
To watch the sunset,
    a spray of the jasmine was put into one's hand

A bouquet,
    more like a child's top or rattle,
Made of the unopened buds of jasmine
    threaded each upon a pine-needle,
And bound with skeins of coloured silk
    into a stick or handle,
A nosegay,
    even a little parachute of jasmine,
Made by the Arab women during the long siesta
    every afternoon

It was a pleasure
    just to hold the jasmine in one's hand
Who, that has known this,
    could forget it,
For in the jasmine is all and everything
    of the Andalucian Moor;
It is a scent, a lovely scent,
    and nothing more at all

Night-Blowing Cereus

Many evenings we looked and waited
For the scented tragedian,
And nothing, nothing,
No blowing of the night-blowing Cereus,
No bursting of the pointed,
Tassell'd calyx
Along the hideous octopus limbs of the cactus,
High above the ocean.

And then on our last evening
All were blowing together,
Some were even opening their petals
While we looked at them;
Huge blossom like a phantom water-lily,

Wholly incredible
In elaboration of your petals,
Of wax-like texture,
Thin as candle-wax that flakes off from the fingers,
The outer flanges folding back
To form the base of the cup or chalice,
A goblet formed of row after row
Of glistening, white flakes or petals;

Scented tragedian, I called you,
Smelling of vanilla,
Ghost and essence
Of moonlight serenade and mantilla,
Not alone, but 'blowing' in tens and dozens
So that the night is tragic,
There is the tragedy of your dying
In the hours before the dawn
Is it all for the fluttering moth,
Night-wanderer,
To be drawn into your snowy chambers
And stay long enough
To become itself the messenger of pregnancy
From flower to flower?
In this one night
You have gone from the bloom of youth
To dishonoured and decrepit age;
The Queen of the Night does not outlive the dawn,
But is quite dead and faded.

The Flowers at Holanducia

Flowers
    taller than the Glass Towers
Beside Lake Michigan,
    and imaginary lilies
Though they are but cockscomb cannas
    The red, and the rough yellow, and the tigered, mottled;
With the pale wonder that opens on the wall
    in the cool of evening
White, green-flanged trumpet
    and climbing parachute that rides the starlight.

There are all the new sorts of bougainvillaea,
    the white, and the rare yellow,
And one which is in tones of apricot and terracotta;
    all bracts, not flowers, if that has meaning,
But growing as easily as sweet peas,
    climbing onto the roof,
And hanging down in festoons over doors and windows,
    next to another climber brought here from the Congo;
A flower that comes new in the morning,
    but one scarcely looks at it because of the 'morning glories'
In the 'drop' or attack they make at dawn,
    some hundreds of the light blue, white-ribbed parachutes
Held still there, neither drifting along the wind,
    nor coming down,
But as in the first moment one saw them in the sky.

    And what more?
Pelargonium-pink
    bignonia, honeyed horns of plenty,
Coming from a part of Mexico where there are sky-blue churches
    with white friezes like clouds upon them;
And in the hibiscus beds
    the humming-birds that you can reach out a hand to touch
Make a soft murmur with their wings
    like the sound of kisses.

Another, and another flower
    that could be a blouse or a shift of rose-coloured satin
With a sulphur-yellow skirt,
    and a diadem of white flowers that quiver
Worn by young Mongolian-looking women;
    or just a huipil,
To those who know the Guatemalan huipil,
    of cadmium-red.

Rose and beige churches
    with violet-coloured domes,
Or maize-colour,
    with tall doors painted in orange tones
And different hues of gold,
    rose-pink, flamingo-coloured,
Selling *huesos de santos* or 'saints' bones' sweets.

With white plumbago,
    or if that other is blue then this is silver,

But in fact it is as white as jasmine, only scentless;
    and there are the geraniums in competition with each other,
For they grow here like groundsel or like dandelions,
    geraniums from all up and down the coast,
Where there is a railwayman's hut at each kilometre
    and you get the quick flash of geraniums, rushing by,
Or from a whitewashed cabin with geraniums at the door,
    and the gardener will bring a rare geranium
Which is a little different from anyone else's,
    and now and again a new break altogether,
One that is the colour of a cyclamen,
    or a geranium striped white and scarlet;
And if I lived here myself
    I would try for Osuna, the town of the Borjas, which is not
      far away,
Where the balconies of the houses 'were ornamented
    with superb carnation pinks' in the time of Richard Ford.

There are innumerable pink and white oleanders
    that the Spaniards call 'adelfas',
And here at the back many hibiscuses are growing,
    probably a white one being the most beautiful of all;
While hereabouts is the pawpaw (papaya) tree,
    the only fruiting one in Europe,
And from here one looks down over the brakes of sugarcane
      across the sea
    to Africa, just where the Riff countrymen
Are un-African with their wide-brimmed, high steeple hats
    of straw, fringed with bobbins of different coloured wools,
And red and white striped clothes,
    more indeed like Chinamen or Koreans in old engravings
From seventeenth-century books of travel.

All, all from Holanducia,
    where time halted,
Stood still a moment and moved on again.

North-Midlands

I am thinking of willowherb
Growing upon a slag-heap

110

And hear the 'penny-engine'
Panting its way through Foxton Wood,
Dragging its feet,
Iron feet,
Cold as the stone guest
At the banquet in *Don Juan*,
Bringing my own ghosts before me
In the old house.

Pink willowherb,
For sweet and sour,
Waving on the slag-heap
Out of the coal dust,
Where children walk into the woods
To pick wild raspberries and red campion.
Ah! lily of the willowherb with Northern accent,
Born of the dark gods of the coalpit,
Miner's daughter and daughter of the hemlock,
From the red brick house with outside lavatory,
Gentle, pale lily of a lifetime,
And fauness of the netted currant-bushes,
Figure of a nymph from off the sea-bed,
Lyre of the ancients, and little golden drudge;
You are going to the slag-heaps
And clinker paths,
Bring them my love!

Snapdragon

Snapdragon,
So proud upon the wall,
We pull down your lip
To listen
As it snaps back again
Without permission.

You cannot of your own will
Open your jaws;
And yet even a child's hand
Plays snapdragon with you;
Your dignity is in perpetual danger.

It is true your flower face
Is a little like a dragon;
So many blind faces
Upon one stem,
And tight-shut dragon jaws;

No stench of dragon breath,
Nothing in your dragon maws,
No smoke, nor fire,
Only your tight-clenched clubber-jaws
And while I look at you
A bee crawls in,
With black velvet forehead
And front pair of claws,
Stays but a moment
And is off again
From snapdragon to snapdragon,
All round the stalk,
For what in a bee's ears
Is but common talk;
Honey cells or honey chambers,
Banks where honey is on safe deposit,
Vaults that open, and then shut behind you,
Unlocked doors that do not bang,
But spring back, soft and deliberate,
Not wood, nor metal,
But with a vegetable clang.

Snapdragons,
You have a foothold
Half-way upon the golden pair of towers
Of El Obradoiro,
Which is the western façade of Compostela,
I have seen you growing there,
Still a weed,
But how proud out of the tawny stone;
I know not what the Spaniards call you,
But you Italian name is *bocca di leone*,
Which means 'lion-mouth';
Both snapdragon and lion-mouth,
Whether by Italian lemon-pot and fountain,
At a statue's foot,
Growing out of a rubbish heap,
Or from the rubble of a red brick wall.

A Look at Sowerby's English Mushrooms and Fungi

As here indeed in five colours in the same drawing
    Of the genus *Russula*, I would guess,
'with domed caps which later become flattened
    and depressed or hollow in the centre';
A little lemony-yellow fungus at bottom of the page,
Near to the eye, yet as a whole solar system of its own,
    and the 'big bang' theory witnessed in very process of
self-creation;
Only an inch from its scarlet neighbour, a flanged galaxy
    still on the umbilical or atomic stalk,
And as though already revolving, spinning
Nearer still—
    how many millions of light years away?—
A mushroom indeed in most of the colours of the rainbow,
Far out across whole aeons of time,
    yet no older or taller than the dandelion;
At foot of a universe in full destruction and decay
Blown outside in, its gills yet functioning,
    as though to say, oceans still heaving,
But rising dangerously,
    and near atop the highest mountains
About to dissolve, disintegrate,
    and go up in dust and vapour
And now among the shadow-fungi,
    Agaricus odorus 'of ratafia odour' for what that means,
Agaricus roseus and *amethystinus*,
    clammy and rubbery as the 'moon-calves' of H. G. Wells;
Thence to mushrooms of more substance,
The fungus *Agaricus tigrinus*,
    of appearance close cousin to a mid-Victorian épergne,
Proferring so many cups or salvers of different sizes
    held out on twisting limbs
On the mahogany table among the regimental silver,
The 'tigerings' all in little scratchings like paw-marks,
    with lesser tiger-cubs among the elder offspring;
And for a different order of sensations
    to *Agaricus monstrosus* found 'in vast abundance
On the left-hand side of the road to Costessy,
    about a mile and a half from Norwich ten years ago',

In presumably 1787,
But in suggestion it could be a pleasure park of modern sculpture
    run up in a night before the fungus-flesh has toughened;
In all contrast to the fly-killer *Agaricus muscarius*
    with shreds of the *annulus* 'beautifully spotting the *pileus*',
Or they can be not so much 'spots' as little warts or warty patches,
    and among the wart-hogs of their ugly family

Yet another composed of an almost infinite number of fine filaments
    which like rags of starlight attach themselves to whatever
    object,
Hence the name *Lycopodus radiatus*,
'Submitted from Holt in Norfolk by the Rev. R. B. Francis
    who found it on the plastered wall of a ball-room;'
And with *Boletus frondosus* we are in the world of monsters,
    toad-like of texture with lateral ramifications,
Branching and re-uniting, more resembling a mollusc,
    even an octopus or cuttlefish than mere fungus

Next to *Phallus impudicus* or *Phallus foetidus*
    the common '*Wood Witch*' or common '*Stinkhorn*',
Less witch than warlock it proclaims itself,
    as in a dormitory competition of evil children;
Or, for another name,
Lacedaemonian Ambassador or *Lacedaemonian Herald*
    as in Beardsley's drawings for *The Lysistrata*;
A fungus that is egg-shaped in its beginnings,
    but like a 'goose's egg' most typically,
Foetid from the thick layer of green jelly
Which attracts the flies to feed upon the slime
    and spread about the spores;
When ripe, the white skin or 'veil' torn
    in monstrous self-circumcision
And erect to full height in a matter of a few hours;
    horned god of the coven

And for like temperament in a fungus
    and the taste of death while it is still alive,
To *Coprinus comatus* or the '*Shaggy Ink Cap*',
A foot and a half tall it can be found
    with the ring or annulus still around the stem;
In youth all in white shaggy scales
    as the fleeced anchorite of a cold Thebaid,
But grown older, the laminations of its cap
    curl upwards at their ends;

114

In advanced state of decay,
    the cap flattened and become rounded
With the gills dropping off,
And dissolving at its edges into a thick, inky fluid;
    now a wheel-mushroom on its tall post or stem,
Reminiscent of the cartwheels with broken bodies still upon them,
Here and there among the gallows
    in more than one of Pieter Bruegel's paintings;
Of more engaging habit,
    those fungi that have grasses growing through them,
Or indeed the grasses are surrounded by them,
    all of a nights' growing,
And must of course draw sustenance from them;
All the same, not quite the toad's embrace
    as when you see a young toad
Riding 'piggyback' upon its parent or grandparent,
    or any old male bull-toad,
    to squeeze the life out of him and make room for others.
But it is a working partnership or *symbiosis*
    between grass and fungus,
'In which both partners benefit'

Now for the Tartar domes of *Lycoperdon proteus*,
    'in many shapes that are hardly to be described',
Seldom being merely globular,
    but shaped like a pear or an onion,
Or bottle-shaped': – and we are in 'Mother-Russia'
    among the churches of a country Kremlin,
Near to the Kitaigorod or 'Chinatown',
With a suburb called Kunavin
    dedicated to pleasure,
With bands and steam-organs,
And blind beggars – the best singers,
Writes Maxim Gorki,
In all Russia—
    bawling in the streets;
These last and their kindred
    being puff-balls, no more or less,
And but one division of them,
    for there are others that are more curious still;
Lycoperdon recolligens a puff-ball that grows underground
    till the volva bursts 'with some elastic force
For they are commonly found tumbled about';
Or Lycoperdon carpobolus on the edge of a tub at Bulstrode,
    in a damp and very hot station in the stove-house

Where grew *Nymphaea nelumbium*,
    the rare aquatic resembling a yellow waterlily
Brought from the East Indies by Sir Joseph Banks

But this puff-ball or *tête de mort* like a *Death's Head Moth*
    has its own noise to make,
Throwing out its white globular part
    'as far as six or eight inches, no more,
With a slight but distinct cracking sound';
Which takes us to those puff-balls
    that from near-to are like little miniature volcanoes,
With the spores or smoke rising from a vent or opening at the top;
Or odder still the 'Earth Star' or *Geastrum triplex*,
    its crater held up on six lobes like lobster claws;
And to another *Geastrum* or *Lycoperdon*,
    that besides being raised up on its six lobes or legs
Has many little pillars or supports to hold up its crater,
    with several orifices to emit the smoke or powder
And we end on a windy day
    with giant puff-balls *Calvatia gigantea*
Coming tumbling, rolling towards us,
    till they lodge among the blackberries,
Under polished green currants of the *'Deadly Nightshade'*.

Pomona

Strawberry Feast

To lift back the net
    above the bed of hautbois strawberries
Is like pulling down the sheet,
    or, better,
There being no coverlet on the bed at all,
But only the girl lying,
    waiting

To pick a strawberry
    is to hold a strawberry in your hand,
Ready for eating,
    with the flecks or sun-motes on its flesh
From what Riviera or Waikiki strand?
    Or rather,
They are straws from the haycocks
    of an earlier, and younger meeting

To eat the strawberries
    from this silver dish
Is to be in company
    with faunesses and nymphs;
The nymph Nausicaa,
    and her with eyes like the auricula,
Who, I have to say,
    is dead

With others, some alive
    and young now,
And others imaginary,
    if not wholly, or not quite,
For whom not death, nor time,
    could dull the appetite

The Pleasure Gardens

For an experience of England
    as strong of its time
As the tapestries of Goya,
    or the Feria of Seville,
Let it be a summer of strawberries and cream
And come walk with me in the pleasure gardens
    to see whom we shall see
. . . and we are past the turnstiles
And under the lantern-lit great trees

That is the roar of London in the distance
    and the lights of London lighting the night sky,
And now we are where there are arbours
    like opera-boxes for eating and drinking,
And men and women speaking our own language
For there is no delight in not being able to talk or understand

The accent is a little strange and different
    if you listen for it,
But here with a crowd following them,
    and as though they are used to that,
Comes the pair of young women
    whom we saw last week or yesterday?

Yesterday or last week? Which was it?
    in the street or at the theatre?
In the huge feathered hats still worn
    by costers' wives or their 'dinahs',
And then the fashion of London,
    last week or yesterday;

Young women of Gainsborough and Rowlandson
    —or Cockneys of Phil May—
In huge hats and wide skirts
    with the hand of Van Dyck still upon them,
Of rain-red skins that give the milk of roses,
    admired at the slangy rooms in Soho Square,
With look of ripe innocence whether from rectory
    or sponging-house,

Now seen eating strawberries and watched by the crowd,
    while a band plays underneath the August trees

Sugar-Ray

To the many who have never seen strawberries growing
    but only bought them from the barrow,
Perhaps in a shower of rain with the water dripping on them
    from a corner of the awning,
You must know that they come close to the earth,
    or upon a straw-matting,
Yes! as a poor family's bed of straw, or the lunatics
    lying on straw in Bedlam;
Then, why are strawberry-leaves the symbol and sign of lords,
    even for Lord Rendal home from the greenwood,
Having drunk the soup of eels stewed in a pan,
    and swelling and dying of poison?
Is it because there are wood-strawberries in the margins of missals,
    with the single pink, and the rose and the periwinkle,
For they coloured and drew the most beautiful things they knew
        on the vellum?

Sweet strawberry, of your own sugar sweetened,
    of sugar radiance and sugar-ray,
Peerless lady of the strawberry bed,
    who was of the ballet, not the ballad world,
And touched the boards with magic,
    but phantom of the green room, not the greenwood,
And come of no line of strawberry-leaves;
    in another life you might have listened to me,
Sweet and dear sugar-ray,
    in the fire tested and of the fiery hair,
And what would have become of us I know not,
    nor by your light of fire do I much care.

Queen Mab Scherzo

Wood-strawberry and silver for whose colours?
And where? And when?
Could it be
    where Cupid made himself a trumpet
From a fallen jacaranda flower,
    and we saw him whisper into the ear of Venus,
And there were golden coaches?
No. No. For that was substantive.
    It was a city.
But this is of Mercutio's telling
    to half-listening Romeo,
Of her, 'drawn with a team of little atomies',
    wood-strawberry and silver her livery and racing-colours;
Her jockeys light as a may-fly upon the weighing scales,
And as blown thistledown within the paddock rails,
Mounted always on a strawberry-roan
    to run against fly-away dandelion,
Lion-mane and lion-mist of the meadows;
Her postilions, ditto, their leaders riding on the off-side;
Their 'cattle', sometimes like the Prince Regent's
    of a bright bay colour, more often strawberry,
Their montero caps sewn, each, from a strawberry-leaf;
Her footmen in strawberry and silver
    with powdered – or could we say
Silvered, or, even, sugared hair
. . . and all from finding a wild strawberry plant

Strawberry Village

(in Japan)

Where are strawberry gardens
    there should be a strawberry village
As unique and beautiful as Ujji,
    the village of green tea;

It should have cottages with high roofs
        of mouse-fur thatch,
And cormorant fishing by torchlight on the river,
Where one need attend but once,
        maybe even a firefly festival

Strawberries of all sorts and kinds
        are on the stalls;
But it is more of a strawberry-tasting,
        and not even that so much
As a strawberry-viewing.
        And where is it to be?
Where a promontory is almost entirely covered
        with strawberry gardens;
The men wear Phrygian caps;
        the women a headdress like that of the goddess Isis,
And the country music is the bagpipe or 'bigniou'?
No. No. Not for all the 'wine of Plougastel'

Preludio

Henry Woodward the harlequin and friend of Garrick,
        buried in the vaults of St George's, Hanover Square,
Dumb witness to many funerals and weddings,
Would come on to soft music,
        sit at a table,
On which there was placed nothing,
And pretend to eat a bunch of currants,
Next, a cherry,
        spurting the cherry-pip from his lips,
Then, all other fruit each in its own way,
        a peach, a gooseberry, or paring an apple,
It was, we are told, an exquisite piece of miming

Mango

As,
    a mango,
Which was something new to him,
Not knowing for the moment what to do with it,
Holding high his hand to look at it all round,
    putting it to his ear,
And shaking it to hear the heavy stone inside

But the mango will not break or split,
    it melts and runs and stains his hand,
Until this harlequin who walked in Bond Street and in Piccadilly,
Is marked with the yellow ichor,
    flesh and lifeblood of the mango,
As though from all four formal plots of mango trees I saw
    where the sister of Aurangzeb lies buried,
And . . . And . .
    Ah! the soft music for the harlequin, I had forgotten—
It would be of birds preening in that more than ilex-shade

'Apples of Messina'

So Nell Gwynne was an orange-girl
    who sold oranges in Drury Lane and Covent Garden,
Moving up and down the stalls,
    in and out of the boxes
And along the balconies,
With the oranges on a tray below a milkmaid's yoke
    slung from her shoulder;
We see her saucy eyes
    and low cut bodice,
And the mamillary-shaped fruit
    the Dutchmen called 'apples of Messina';
And soon this 'impudent comedian'
    from the theatre smelling of orange-peel

Is having 'familiar discourse' with the King
    and his spaniels,
'Looking out of her garden on a terrace at the top of the wall . . .
    and standing on the green walk below it'

The harlequin, also,
    is no stranger to Drury Lane or Covent Garden;
But it sets me thinking of cloisters I have known
    planted with orange trees,
And smelling of orange blossom;
Scents of Araby, most surely,
    and from further away still,
Where loquat and cumquat
    are full breast midgets in a land of bantams
Ah, give Woodward the harlequin
    an orange to suck,
And he will bring us in a breath
    back from the bantam land to Cockney London

Tangerine

When shops are lit,
    sleet falls in the Midlands
And it is cold without and in,
I am back at the white columns of the Cappuccini
    with the long stairway leading down to the sea,
Listening to the Sicilienne!
On a December afternoon with the frost beginning,
    with the zampognari coming,
And frost upon the tangerines,
Hearing the bagpipes of the shepherds
    come up from Calabria for the novena,
Music, as of goatskins with the hair on,
    filled with wind,
Listen! how it skirls from its own entrails,
    and how the drone goes on,
Rough hairy music, but it is the Sicilienne!

I connect it in my memory
    with frost upon the black-green leaves,
And lit lanterns of the tangerines,

When I was young,
    and dreaming often of the temples of Angkor,
And from my window at Amalfi
    looking across the sea to Spain,
Having begun, then, to write a book
Of Habaneras and Siciliennes

Knowing, now, there is a link
    between this music and the London theatres,
For Handel had heard the shepherds' bagpipes,
    the zampognari or the pifferari,
Bagpipes by either name
So hand Woodward a tangerine,
    and hear the castrato's voice in it,
Watch fields of anemones and asphodels
    see the Barbary pirates and their feluccas,
And the waves sliced thin,
    and be in London and in Sicily
With the harlequin

'La Reine Claude'

In memory of my darling Georgia

There is a red brick cottage
    on the steep hill of Lois Weedon,
With a greengage tree,
The cottager has spoilt it all,
    rebuilt the cottage,
Yet kept the greengage tree,
And still on an August evening
You could see the plum branches
    against the cloudless sky,
And think the scented hand
Lay on the windowsill,
And that the green eyes of La Reine Claude
    looked in the window
When it is too dark to see distinctly,
    Time is like that:
It has no sympathy

Ah! my companion and my love
	through many difficulties,
If we could but sleep the winter
	through all the centuries;
But it changes everything,
	till there is nothing left
Where we lived happily,
	Time is like that:
It has no pity and no sympathy

And yet,
	my greengage,
My pledge of love and my security,
You would not have it otherwise
Than that it is ours alone
	for all eternity;
I'll lend the harlequin your soft cheek to kiss,
	my shadow and my ghost,
And Time that has no pity
	takes another meaning and new emphasis

Blackberrying

I am of mind to go blackberrying
	which it is a pity to do alone
One should always have companions for fruit-picking:—
So choose them carefully,
	there are the living to choose from,
Or you can choose them from the dead

It is a foraying into forgotten fields,
	some of them not seen for years on end,
And we could set forth in any of two or even three directions:—
	to the long spinney with a pond in the middle of it,
Or beyond that in the distance to the wood called Grumbler's Holt
	which means a bear had his lair there many hundred years ago,
A dead tramp was found in it some weeks back
	without his trousers,
And the police must draw their own conclusions;
	giving a feeling, even a meaning to the wood
Which in truth it had already,
	ever since I remember it

Or to the Armada Fields as we call them,
  beyond the old manor with that tell-tale date above the window:—
We choose the latter
  and soon begin to work along the hedges

To about where on that winter day,
  I so well remember,
While I was at work on *A Look at Sowerby's English Mushrooms and Fungi*,
  the giant dead puff-balls*
Came tumbling, rolling towards us
  like child-clowns in some nightmare circus,
Till they lodged just exactly here among these blackberries

Which do not compare to the more Northern blackberries of Foxton
  Wood,
  as a North Countryman myself I like to think:—
Childhood memories of which still work on me with a little tightening of
  the heart,
  and more still the taste of the little wild raspberries of the same wood
For the sharpness of their bite and rasp,
Of intent for whom? Surely of satyric,
  goat-haunch satisfaction and satiety,
I am thinking

It could be true that the further North you go
  the better are the wild berries,
Attaining to their best in Lapland and in Finland;
Always remembering that extraordinary breakfast at half-past six in the
  morning,
  at Bodø in Norway, just north of the Arctic Circle,
The dishes of unknown yellow or red berries
  with bowls of para-paradisal white, white milk;
Having flown past the Lofoten Islands lying off to the right,
  like an unimaginable, unattainable vision of Leonardo's,
Lasting out maybe for more than a hundred miles of ocean;
  and wondering what life could be like there;
Were there early frescoed churches as on the Aland Islands in the
  Baltic?
  There are certainly the wondrous wild flowers
And a peculiar breed of dog the Lofoten Seal Hound!
We had been to see two villages of Lapps,
  Kautokeini and Rovaniemi,
But only the Lappish women were there,
  the men had gone down to the sea with their reindeer herds;

* *Calvatia gigantea.*

126

We only saw the women and children and the huge dogs.
Yes! It was at Bodø where the Norwegian ex-naval officer
        of long experience in the Arctic
Came aboard the yacht to arrange the salmon fishing
        in the Alten-Fjord;
And walking with me in the town
        past a shop hung with huge polar bearskins that reached from floor
    to ceiling

Told me he could never shoot another polar bear:—
        this was after he had watched one of them
At sight of a human being
Shamble away holding up a paw
        to hide the black patent-leather end to its nose,
The one patch of black in all the whiteness of the snow scene
        which made the bear vulnerable:—
I had never thought to find myself talking to someone
        with knowledge of Nova Zembla and Spitzbergen

Blackberrying is maybe our nearest equivalent
        to the *vendemmia* or grape-picking,
And hence the need for pleasing companions,
For Swanilda,
        with eyes I said like the auricula,
Embodiment of the pearlshell hour and first breath of morning;
Swanilda,
        who used to read my poems in the Tube,
Whom I apostrophised as Madonna of the Shoal of Pearls,*
My memory of her is still inhabitant of the Madonna dell'Orto:—
        though dead these thirty years,
Now gone for ever into the lagoon of time

And we come down along one of the most far off, most distant of the
    hedges
        with a basketful of the most bacchic-looking of the blackberries,
Clusters that spill out their staining ichor
        so that it is like the slaughtered death bed of the berries,
So heavy the basket that we take it in turn to carry it,
        and it dyes even the dead leaves on the ground
If we put it down for a moment

* Dict.: 'apostrophe, a turning away from the subject of a speech, to address someone', and
it adds, significantly, 'present or absent'.
    This poem is dedicated to Pearl Argyle, most lovely of all ballerinas (1910–47).

Medlar, or Mespilus germanica

Medlar is a name lone-standing and aloof
    which is the character of *Mespilus germanica*,
Though why indeed that qualification
    for the medlar is met with more in Turkey and in Asia Minor?

A fruit tree of reticence which loves not its neighbours
    but likes to withdraw into itself,
And has even its own verb to 'blet'
    implying the medlars must not be picked until the frost has
'bletted' them

And most decidedly a taste and flavour of its own
    as though murmuring 'medlar', 'medlar' while it is in your mouth
So that you will recognise and always remember it,
    for it does not in fact so often come one's way,
Which is a reason in itself for planting medlars:—
They like to stand by themselves of preference in a neglected corner
    making a brave show in autumn with their coats of leaves
That scarce rattle in a wind so close the golden lappets

And when it comes to picking, or in fact collecting medlars
    which bruise so easily as they lie upon the ground,
When they are cracked by frost and in fact and indeed 'bletted',
    it will be difficult to believe how delicate will be the flavours,
Subtler, more interesting than their cousin quince
    for both quince and medlar are classified as *rosaceae*

The reticence being that medlars do not invite you to bite into them,
    but reserve themselves for more considered and delayed eating,
Indeed in particular circumstances as with a glass of good red wine,
    no apple-chewing as with the whistling errand-boy,
But only when sitting by the warm fireside;
Or as at the moment when the country gods lift up their cups
    to toast Pomona, 'a nymph of Rome',
The goddess of all sorts of fruit trees
    and who, like it, or like it not,

'Disdained the toils of the field and the fatigues of hunting,'*
    to keep herself for Vertumnus, deity of autumn and of all orchards,
  inclusive of course of medlars

Mulberry, or Morus

How? Oh! how could George Peele have thought of
'God in the whizzing of a pleasant wind
Shall march upon the tops of mulberry trees'
    It is one of the major, minor miracles of poetry
By a minor poet,
Remembering, as well, the sad tragical history
    'under a white mulberry tree, without the walls of Babylon',
Which gave the mulberry immortality
Twice over, in the legend and in the play,
    and after that what more is there to say of mulberries?

What more is there to say?
    Except that in most old gardens there is a mulberry tree
With always some sentiment attaching to it:—
Not least for myself in a very old and neglected garden.
    below the garden at my childhood home,
A garden made perhaps a hundred and fifty years ago
    for a Scots great-grandmother;
And always run down and through by my brother and myself
    in our summer holidays on the way down to the lake.
And in one of the agonies of childhood,
It would be in the second or third week of September,
    going our hateful different ways to school
For we were never at school together;
In our misery at the separation,
    for twelve weeks is a long time for a child,
We buried something, I forget what, under the mulberry tree
    in token of our love for each other,
It could have been a pair of cuff-links,
    which I suppose must still be there:—
To this day it upsets me and I do not like to think of it,
    after all that there has been,
And so much that has happened since

* Cf Dr Lempriere, D.D.

Tropical Fruit-Picking

What a pity never to have had experience
    of tropical fruit-picking!
Only to have watched early in the morning
    the melon barges on the Klongs of Bangkok:—
The fruit stalls of Cuernavaca
    selling grenadillas, sapotes,
    mangoes and papayas:—
And the wayside fruit-sellers of Taprobane,
    which is the lovelier name for Sri Lanka;
Their pineapples as big as fire-buckets,
Ten or fifteen sorts and kinds of bananas,
    and mangoes and mangosteens

In default of which having written some fifty poems for *Tropicalia*,
    eleven of them on the frangipani
Among the most lovely flower visions of the tropics;
Many allusions to my admiration for the jacaranda;
    to 'that scented tragedian'
Night-blowing Cereus,
    with tribute after tribute to the double flowering hibiscus

And a long poem
    'On Listening to Music under Tropical Flowering Trees'
Where I imagined all sorts of tropical floral accompaniments
    to listening to music by the Masters;
And yet another poem 'The Flowers at Holanducia'
On a garden in Spain with a pawpaw (papaya tree)
    'the only fruiting one in Europe'.

And there too,
'The pale wonder that opens on the wall
    in the cool of evening,
White, green-flanged trumpet
    and climbing parachute that rides the starlight,'
'Next to another climber brought here from the Congo
    a flower that comes new in the morning,
But one scarcely looks at it because of the "morning glories"
In the 'drop' or attack they make at dawn,
    some hundreds of the light blue, white-ribbed parachutes

Held still there, neither drifting along the wind,
    not coming down,
But as at the first moment one saw them in the sky'

Remembering so well the hibiscus
    in a friend's garden at Lima in Peru,
And at Casa Contenta so well named
    on Lake Atitlán in Guatemala;
They were the newest hibiscus hybrids from nurseries in Hawaii;
A double rose,
    a satiny yellow,
        a yellow flushed with scarlet,
A cinnamon-coloured, almost a sandalwood hibiscus

Having written so many poems to the hibiscus
    as to the jacaranda,
So that at least if I have had no experience of tropical fruit-picking
    I have delved quite deeply among the wonders of the tropical
flower garden,
With initiation among the flowers and flowering trees of Funchal
    which indeed for surpass in beauty their equivalents in the
Caribbean:—

As ready to write a poem to the rose as to the auricula,
    to the lily as to the 'flaming' and 'feathering' of the tulip,
In all of which I have been to some little extent participant,
    as in the rescuing of a few forgotten and forsaken flowers

Black Apricot

And returning once more
    for farewell to this autumn's fruit-picking,
What a fascination it is to read of *Prunus dasycarpa*,
A cross it seems between apricot and myrobolan or cherry plum,
    'fruits black with a purple bloom, apricot-flavoured
Rarely produced in the British Isles.
And known as the Purple or Black Apricot',
    which like the greengage adds another dimension to the mere
plum tree,
For the Black Apricot should be treasured possession of a necromancer
    grown maybe in the garden of Nostradamus,

Of the red-bearded Sephardim,
    but coming from Salon near Avignon,
And of as sinister a reputation as the more notorious Doctor Faustus

Japonica, or Cydonia

But all good things must have their ending
    and this is a farewell to another autumn,
Though no more than fruit-picking in a walled garden;
    this afternoon it is the yellow japonica-apples we are after,
Or call them chaenomeles or more simply just cydonia;
    but by whichever name just listen
To the little snap of the fruit-stalk:—
    it breaks off in a way of its own
As though to assert an individuality
    and to say 'we have as good,
Or better a way of doing it'

Coming in fact from the other side of the world
    which was a six month's voyage not long ago,
Soon after that a month or more,
    and now a longish night of fourteen hours;
And it would be disappointing
    if most things even now were not a little different
As are the complexions of japonica apples,
    the red, red marks like stains upon their yellow skins
While other sorts of japonicas have the most unripe-looking apples
    ever seen,
    but most are large yellow quinces more correctly called
There being some thirty or more varieties or *cultivars* to choose from
    grown chiefly for their flowers:—
Deeper crimson, rich vermilion, clear scarlet, salmon-pink,
    but only a few growers can be bothered to make jelly from them

So back to the Derbyshire hill country
    and that rail-ridden though still green valley,
Below the magical, most magical Bolsover
    which was to me the school of poetry:—
Woods where I first perceived what a wood should be,
Grass I thought to be
    the green of a mermaid's or of the nereid's hair,

And bluebells of course
     almost to satiety
But where? oh! where
     the fauness of the netted currant-bushes?
For the scene is not whole and entire without her,
Who came from the same steep slopes
     down to the woods and collieries;
And who minds the chugs or trugs for our fruit-picking,
     another more pliant Charpillon of the sensual netting,
Little familiar spirit,
     and fauness none the less

'Look not for Silvanus'

Look not for Silvanus in a wood of deodars,
     Himalayan cedars that scent the mountain winds;
Among the date palms; or in the 'red-wood' trees
     their shade as tall along the hillside as pyramids of Egypt;
While Silvanus in spirit is alien to the quincentennial oak-trees,
     with their past that goes back far but not far enough in time

Think not of Silvanus in the yew-tree's shade
     with an owl for watchman,
There is nothing of the Druid in his ancestry,
     of goat-blood and of pagan past;
Silvanus would abhor both standing stones and burial mounds,
     the circle of monoliths is not for him,
Neither the stylite on his column, nor the stone-cold cromlech

His magic is for warmer and more southern moods
     where nightingales are singing in the wood of cypresses,
With oranges,
     not apples on the autumn trees:—
And even the hibiscus getting warmer still
     for flower to be worn behind the ear;
Not here the gentian
     the thrush-throat gentian,
Remembering the first time I found one
     on a hillside in the Abruzzi,
And then a dozen, then hundreds a whole covey of them,
     with a lark singing as though in pride of it
In the empty blue egg-shell sky

A Bestiary of Birds and Beasts

Poetic Exercise in the Form of a Fight With a Giant Bird

Lost lost
On the borders of Campeche and Quintana Roo
Among serpent mounds and cast-off sloughs of serpents
Where once was a huge city
Lost lost
Myself
Turning from side to side
And cannot sleep
Losing losing
The lost world
Looking for other worlds
And but man-sent mice and monkeys
Shot up come down
Found

Lost
Mayan city
Whose great men were astronomers
Who worshipped time
Tall stone stela
Fallen face down
Lost lost
Me
Myself
Till hell is this jungle
With brain running too fast
Or slowing down

All at once
In the black hell of doubt
Where I toss and turn
In the glare of mid-day
In middle of the dead town
A wind-strumming noise

Wind going through slats and feathers
Quills or pinions flapping drily
And we look up into the air

Who? Or what is it?
The cacique and star-numberer
From the stone stela
With sloping forehead and malformed head?
But we look up into the tree-tops
And a huge bird
With a seven or eight foot wing-spread
With wings as big in my bedroom
As a four-poster bed

A white King vulture
Now in the crown of a very tall tree
Dead white with black wing tips
And multicoloured head
Vulture face with patches of paint like pigment on it
Bright red curved beak
Set into a jet-black base
Long neck and yellow wattles
Sparse long hair
That is the horror of it
On an otherwise bald head
King of the carrion-eaters
Sarcorhamphus Papa

In my dream
I take a gun and fire at it
But the vulture but shook itself
And a full half-minute later
Falls
Down through the branches
But rights itself
And goes off into a steep glide
Next seen
Standing in an open clearing
And I fire again straight into its head
But incredibly
The bloody-headed monster begins running

And now the killing is done for me by the dead man
Who runs after it
Diving for its feet

Grabbing at one of its yellow horny-scaled legs
Now the bloody wattles and part of the naked head
The hottest vilest head
Are held hard in his hand
And they are rolling over and over together on the ground
With its wings beating against his face
Old Sarcorhampus Papa stank
As could only the King of the world's carrion-eaters
Vomiting all over him
While it sank one of its feet
Shod with long claws
Into his thigh

At last he got one leg
Across those beating wings
And twisted its two-foot snake-like
Neck back back
But instead of snapping
The carrion-eater only fought the harder
Hissing
With tongue darting out of its beak
While he pounded its boa-neck
Three inches thick
And smashed its skull upon a rock

It fought back like a fighting-cock
Kicking and jabbing with its needle claws
Into his upper legs
But using its beak as a lever
He twisted its neck round with both hands
And though he could not break it
Got out his knife
And slid the seven-inch steel blade
Into the bird's soft guts
Only then did it relax
Sarcorhamphus Papa ha! ha!
Was dying dying
Dead
And he sliced off its two enormous breasts
Of meat that stank
And wiping his bloody hands
On its vomit-stained white feathers
Went back to find his friend was dead

'Tzintzuntzin'

The 'Indians' of the stepped pyramids
    and sloping foreheads,
Who wore cloaks of feathers,
Had the word 'tzintzuntzin' for the humming-birds,
    which means 'tresses of the day-star'
This,
    from a race whose priests were astronomers,
And had deduced there were 'day-stars'
From the sun and moon shining together
    in daylight at opposite ends of the sky;
In the sense that 'day-stars' were high in the empyrean,
    drifting in galaxy:
Or were messengers for something invisible,
    or not yet in sight,
And that the heavens were alive with rushing bodies,
    as of every humming-bird upon the wing at once

Bee-Eaters

The blue flash of the bee-eaters
    of the telegraph wires,
And the spreading or clapping of their wings
Of brown or terracotta,
    showing the colour underneath,
And they are all gone like the blue flash of lightning

At the wooden abbey of the iris screen;
    blue irises,
With a stage at one end of the 'Stork Chamber',
Never long enough to see the play,
    down corridors of warm scented cedar,
With monkeys painted upon the grain

And where cycads explode out of the earth
    like rockets

As in the 'Tiger-Garden',
And there are ferns and sago-palms;
A few moments only,
        and no more

At the pavilion built out into the blue lotuses,
        blue waterlilies,
I would not stay longer than a night or two;
Not, there, nor at Lake Atitlán,
But only for long enough to watch the humming-birds,
        and then home

To a Yellow Parrot of Amazon (in London)

1

Bird
        of uncertain sex,
Henbird or cockbird, no one knows,
        uncaged, and *en poste* in Belgrave Square;
Saffron masquer,
        cackling
But its own name 'papagei'!
        as it perches on a shoulder in the bathroom

It is to have inhabited another world
        to know a land of parrots,
Yellow parrot of Amazon,
        or Mato Grosso,
Mocker and inspirer
        of the soft *modinhas* of Brazil:
'Languid, interrupted measures,
        as if the breath was gone with excess of rapture,
And the soul panting to meet the kindred soul,'
        so Beckford wrote,
Hearing a band of oboe and flute players posted at a distance
        in the thicket of orange and bay trees in the gardens of
        Queluz

Your yellow breast and wings,
    here in London,
Pale yellow with no green in them,
    rarest of colours,
No living parrot of your livery,
    nor yellow parrotess within five thousand miles,
Tell of an Indies vanished, that has never been

Parrot-paragon
    of a tree or two in a patch of forest
Which is your habitat,
Bird-brother
    to the yellow lily-trees of Polannaruwa,
Celestial being, if of raucous tongue
    which speaks
Yet speaks not, for it has no sense

While that other,
    your sister-flower above the 'sleeping' Buddha,
Not asleep,
    but in Nirvana which is beyond death,
'Yet not being dead is substantive,'
    of its beauty
Promises oblivion in the Master's name

It is better to know there is no more to come,
    who have no religion, and am but pagan;
Your yellow wings and breast are enough,
Harbinger and beaked halcyon;
    one must not ask too much of either life or death,
Bright mirror of fewer cares and worries,
Messenger
    of the mauve airs of the jacaranda

Parrot-Pie

In the towns of wooden shacks
    a favourite dish was parrot-pie;
Not parrots in pie-crust,
    or a cold half-eaten parrot-pie

But always of the yellow-bellied parakeet,
    common as starlings in Trafalgar Square,
Yellow head and belly with a long blue tail,
    a rudder tail
To steer it through the pungent, eucalyptus'd air

Blue wings and green parrot-back,
    a red clown's mask with blue cheeks,
Some scarlet tigerings upon its yellow front,
    now plucked and gutted, and in the cooking-pot

Which had wings and tail of lazuline,
    wore lapis lazuli and had a yellow breast;
All gone this hundred years
    the showering comets
That lit the streets of Adelaide

On a Toad in a Bed of Lilies-of-the-Valley

What a life
    the toad led for two summers
Living and sleeping in the bed of lilies-of-the-valley
And then,
    on a morning like any other he was gone!
Was he
    the same as the toad in the coal-cellar,
Or another?

Not a tramp
    asleep under a haystack,
This toad in the wood or spinney
    of lilies-of-the-valley,
But the vagabond and black-faced mezzetin
    of the casual ward
—unshaven tramps have mezzetin's black mask—
Awakened under the jacaranda,
Looking up at the blue flowers,
    and collecting a few sticks together
To build a fire

Squatting there
     all day on his haunches,
Unblinking,
     hardly moving,
Inhaling and exhaling
Inspiring and suspiring
     on the lilied air

Little Cavalier

The little dog barked all night long
     at the tiger-lilies;
Who would look for an aesthete
     in a lap-dog's eyes?

The Climacteric

The climacteric,
    a climacteric, no less,
With another birthday only a week ahead
    and nearly a lifetime of failure
If not wholly unsuccess:
    so little of time left
And the summing-up still hot upon the printing-press:—

Oh! stay with me, my Muse,
    and do not leave me
With my family skeletons around me:—
    a father and a mother
My sister and my brother